HELENA DAVIES

Travels of a War Baby

Eight decades of eventful family life
and a passion for travel

Mereo Books

2nd Floor, 6-8 Dyer Street, Cirencester, Gloucestershire, GL7 2PF
An imprint of Memoirs Books. www.mereobooks.com
and www.memoirsbooks.co.uk

Travels of a war baby

978-1-86151-613-8

First published in Great Britain in 2021
by Mereo Books, an imprint of Memoirs Books.

A CIP catalogue record for this book is available from the British Library.

The address for Memoirs Books can be
found at www.mereobooks.com

Mereo Books Ltd. Reg. No. 12157152

Typeset in 11/15pt Century Schoolbook
by Wiltshire Associates.
Printed and bound in Great Britain

To my grandchildren
and great-grandchildren

Preface

During this time of horror, when the world is facing the coronavirus, I have turned my thoughts to my early childhood, as I was born into a world quite different from that of today. It was a world filled with terror of another type of warfare – one which also killed many, but in a different yet horrible way.

One of the biggest differences between then and now is how society and our expectations of what is 'normal' have changed. The way the average person lived then was hugely different from today – expectations were much lower, the pace of life much slower – but what has not changed is what holds us all together, our care for each other, human interaction, and love. Sadly, the greatest difference is that the current pandemic is forbidding human interaction and I wonder if the world will ever be quite the same. Kissing on cheeks? Shaking hands? For the present, all gone; let us just hope that one day soon they will return.

In February 1941, Glamorganshire was savagely bombed, killing 230 people over three days; on the 14th of November of that year, Coventry was devastated by massive bombing attacks which lasted until the morning of November 15th. Buildings were flattened and 530 people killed, necessitating mass graves being dug. Into this world of terror and fear, hatred, and loss I was born – apparently at lunchtime – on the 16th of November, 1941.

My father was, like many, serving during the war. He was in the army, as was his brother, who was killed in Greece. Four of my mother's brothers were also serving their country. Two were radio officers in the Merchant Navy, involved in escorting conveys of ships; one was driving tanks through Italy and involved in the fighting there, whilst one, Lyn, was in the Royal Navy and was a gunner on the *Hermes*, sadly killed aged 22 when it was torpedoed on April 9th 1942, off the coast of Sri Lanka (then Ceylon).

Lyn had spent most of his childhood living with my great grandparents. There he had experienced the consequences of World War 1, as their son Harry also lived there and sadly, he still suffered badly from shell shock. I was told that Harry could not even drink a full glass or cup of liquid – he shook too much. Having experienced these horrors, when Lyn was conscripted into the army he refused to go, dreading the thought of being shell shocked. So afraid was he that my grandfather went to Swansea with him to the enlisting centre, explained the situation and Lyn was transferred to the Royal Navy. Ironically, he was the only one of the four sons in the war to be killed.

So it was a violent and often tragic world, but one in which people appreciated things that are taken for granted today. Food and clothing were on ration and sweets and sugar were scarce, but many people, like my maternal grandfather, grew vegetables in an allotment and kept chickens to provide fresh eggs.

The first five years of my life were lived in a place called Baglan. Now a suburb of the South Wales steel town of Port Talbot, in those days it was a small village set in lovely countryside and with moors leading down to the miles of sandy beach at the coastline.

The only stories I have heard about my babyhood were from my mother and her sister, May, who was fourteen when I was born. My mother and I lived in what was commonly referred to, and literally meant, 'two rooms'. With husbands away fighting and little or no money, many women lived in rented accommodation such as this. In our case, the other 'two rooms' of the house were occupied by another such wife and baby. We were advantaged in that my maternal grandparents lived only a few doors away, so most of our time was spent there.

The only story from my mother relating to me as a baby was that I was 'ugly'. She used to tell me that she hated it when people asked to look in the pram, and that my great grandmother Emily Llewellyn had said 'do not worry, she is like the ugly duckling and will grow into a beautiful swan'. I think this must have been wishful thinking on her side, as I am certainly no swan, but perhaps I have reasonable looks!

The other story, from May, was how she used to come down to our accommodation at night and sleep in the double bed with my mother. May would sleep at the side of my cot and told me that I would not sleep unless someone was holding my hand – consequently May's hand was fixed permanently between the bars of my cot, holding my hand, whilst her own got very cold! I have often thought, in later years, how un-maternal my mother's feelings must have been towards me, that she chose not to lie alongside her baby. I have also thought how much – even at that early age – love and social interaction meant to me.

Two other stories I was told: one was that when there was an air raid, I was always put in the cupboard under the stairs; secondly that when they went onto the mountain in order to collect whinberries, which later would be baked into a delicious pie or – a Welsh 'tart' (the Welsh word for a pastry pie/dish), I would be placed amongst the ferns and guarded by our lovely German Shepherd, Rex.

Contents

CHAPTER 1

My earliest years

I look back on my early childhood with great fondness and huge love for my grandparents, with whom I spent all my time. My memories crowd in like whirling snowflakes in a blizzard, with no particular shape or chronological order. They seem rather like the poem 'I remember, I remember...' I remember my bedroom, which was the box room in my grandparents' house. The next bedroom was occupied by three of my uncles, Roy, Malcolm, and Ralph. Ralph was only eight years older than me, the others not much more. On a Sunday morning my grandmother would come into my bedroom at about 7.30 carrying a cup of tea, which she would place on the bedside table. 'Grandma's going to church now, be a good girl until I come back,' she would say. So often, once she had gone, I would get out of bed and go into the boys' bedroom. Here I would have stories told to me, often made up by one or another of my uncles, and sometimes there were pillow fights – which were great fun!

Of course, food was rationed during and after the war, and on Sunday mornings, after my gran had returned from church, the table would be laid for breakfast. I cannot remember what I ate, but I remember that my grandfather (who always sat at the head of the table) always received the much coveted – and sparse – bacon. How we remember the tiniest, most insignificant things and forget the big occasions!

I remember that he always put vinegar on his bacon, and carefully cut off the rinds. When he had finished (I would be looking longingly at his plate), I would ask if I could have the rinds. We always had plenty of eggs, as we kept chickens in a coop at the back of the garden. We also always had fresh vegetables, as below our road was a large field which had been turned into allotments. The first allotment you reached was my grandfather's and I remember helping to carry down the waste, cabbage stumps, potato peelings etc, and he (I called him Dad Charlie – his name was Charles) would put the waste into a trench he had dug specifically to house these items until they turned into rich compost. He always had a motor bike, and I also remember the odd days when he would go out early in the morning and return with a lot of delicious mushrooms which he had collected, and we would then sit down to a feast of a breakfast.

A very comforting memory of my bedroom was the gentle hiss of the gas light. We had no electricity until about 1947, so cooking and lighting were done by gas. Over the light was fixed a sort of shade called a mantle and alongside the light was a switch that allowed the gas to be raised or lowered. I can remember my gran dimming the light above my bed, and I would fall asleep to the gentle hiss of the lamp. I also remember the sound of the gas lights in church, and the squeaking noise made when one of the choir boys pumped the organ for the organist. Things are all so different now.

Wash day

My grandmother kept to the old routine of doing all the week's washing on Monday mornings. Adjoining the kitchen, they had added what in those days was commonly called a 'lean-to'. Basically, it was another room, with a plastic roof, which accommodated all my grandmother's laundry accoutrements. I think she must have had some sort of washing machine, but I also remember her using a doily (it was used to pummel the clothes and extract dirt), and then she used a mangle, basically a machine with rollers at the top; the clothes were fed between the rollers to remove all excess water. On dry days this was brought outside, as it then gave more room for heavy sheets etc. to be stretched out and placed through the mangle. This was where I came in: I would stand on the outside and catch the sheets as they came through, ensuring that they did not drop onto the ground.

Between the back path and the garden was a low wall, and I loved to sit on that and talk to our lovely Alsatian, Rex. During the war and for some years after, women would have to make alterations to recipes, eg powdered eggs were used for cooking instead of fresh. My grandmother also used condensed milk, which was VERY thick and VERY sweet. No one seemed to be diet or calorie conscious in those days, and whenever my gran was cooking, I would beg for the empty condensed milk can. I was elated when I got it, and quickly got a teaspoon, sat on the little wall outside the kitchen, and scraped every morsel out of that tin!

Other 'sweet' memories of this time relate to a boy, Donald, who was about my age and lived opposite. I remember going into his house and his Mum making sweets (she must have used condensed milk). I know that the sweets tasted wonderful, and she parcelled them into small blue sugar bags. Perhaps readers would not know that in those days sugar was always sold in distinctive blue bags.

Another memory I have is of when Donald and I used to go fishing for 'tiddlers'. At the bottom of the allotment field ran a stream and fishing here was a great adventure. You would think we were going far away, as the trip always necessitated a picnic. This usually consisted of two pieces of bread, thinly spread with sugar (ugh!) and a bottle of water. Then, armed with our jam jars fitted with carrying string, we would set off, and return several hours later after having a splendid time and carefully carrying the jam jar filled with tiddlers.

Kind neighbours

I can never remember my grandmother going into neighbours' houses, nor any of them coming into our house, yet everyone spoke to everyone else, and all were friendly towards each other. When we lived (or should I say 'slept') in the rented two rooms, our next-door neighbours were Mr and Mrs Garlick. I have such fond memories of them! They had two daughters, Joan and Myrna, both of whom were older than me, and as is quite usual of younger children, I thought they were both magnificent and hero-worshipped them. One of the toys I longed to have was a doll's pram (I don't think I even had a doll). Such presents, unless you were EXTRAORDINARILY rich, were unheard of in wartime, but Mr Garlick, whom I called 'Daddy' Garlick, rallied around and made me a slatted wooden doll's pushchair as compensation for having no pram. He painted it pale blue and proudly presented it to me. He was SO kind. Sadly, I never let on, but I was secretly disappointed in my gift – the reason being that Daddy Garlick was unable to make round wheels and the wooden wheels were hexagonal, resulting in a very loud noise when moved! I must have looked and sounded like a member of the Flintstone family whenever I tried to push it!

I distinctly remember that on a Saturday, when all the children were out playing in the road (quite safe as hardly anyone had cars), we would all rush in to the Garlicks' kitchen to listen to the weekly episode of 'Dick Barton, Special Agent', a serial which started in 1946. It was broadcast every evening and then the whole week's episodes could be heard on Saturday morning. Such happy memories!

Saturday evenings

This was probably one of my favourite times, when my grandmother and I could have our 'special' time together. The boys that were still at home would be going out, either to meet girlfriends or to find them at a local dance! Going out in those days meant a white shirt, collar and tie. The collars were separate from the shirts and stiffly starched – my grandmother washed the shirts, but took the collars to the Chinese laundry, which was a shop run by a Chinese family in Aberavon, near the old market.

I forgot one important piece of information – my grandparents had eleven children, nine boys and two girls (my mother, Helen, and May, her sister). I am amazed that my grandmother had enough love and patience to shower some on me – she truly was an angel!

Back to Saturday evening. The stiffly starched collars (all marked on the inside with individual names) were kept in an old biscuit tin which showed Coronation photos of King George and Queen Mary. Routinely my gran would hand out the correct collar to each boy. The boys would duly leave, soon followed by my grandfather, who went to meet male friends at the Conservative Club.

After the noise and the hustle and bustle, a tranquil peace would descend and after I had bathed my grandmother would sit on the settee, with me snuggled up to her and the radio would be put on for 'Saturday night theatre', one of my grandmother's favourite programmes. It was a special time for us, a time for cuddles and togetherness. Of course, I would get tired and fall asleep in her arms. I would then remain on the settee until one of the 'boys' (my uncles) came home. The first one in had the task of carrying me up to my bed.

The other thing I remember about Saturday nights was having my hair washed. It was my grandmother's desire for me to have curly hair. To force my locks into ringlets, she would wind them into 'rags'. 'Rags,' I can almost hear you say, 'what are rags?' That is literally what they were – strips of white cotton which were wrapped in a certain way to enclose the hair into rolls. I suppose they were the predecessors of hair rollers! The following morning they would be undone, and my hair would cascade into curls. Sadly, they did not remain for long, and after several attempts the rags were abandoned.

Other 'special' days I had with my grandmother all to myself was when she would give me a huge treat and take me to the

TINY cinema in Briton Ferry. It really WAS tiny, and I think the upstairs accommodated six people! My gran loved the old music hall songs and would often hum them whilst working, but she also loved Fred Astaire and Ginger Rogers, and I must admit, I still admire them today. I think it was due to them that I started to dance, standing on top of the dining table when no one was around. I can also remember being caught by one of my uncles when I almost fell off!

My final memories of these early years were walking with other children to a small farm which was located up a short road opposite the vicarage. In the front of the farmhouse was a small room which had been turned into a shop – It was known as Civils' farm, as the owner's surname was Civil. It was here that the locals bought their bread. I loved going with the older children to fetch our loaf, but I often had to hide part of it when I got back as it was so tempting to pull off lumps of the bread as we walked home!

On the way to the farm, we would walk past the duck pond which was opposite the vicarage. Here I could talk to the ducks whilst standing on the small wall and holding on to the steel railings which joined each stone pillar. Those steel rails (they were more like circular tubes) also ran along all the house fronts in our road, did not remain long. I distinctly remember men coming and removing them as they were all used for the war effort, steel being in short supply for bullets, explosive shells etc.

These early years spent in my grandparents' house were so happy. You could not get toys, and dolls, dolls' prams etc were unavailable; there were no swings, no parks to play in, but we had fields and streams, rope swings hanging from big oak trees, ferns to hide in on the mountains, and woods where we could imagine fairies and gnomes... what more could a child want?

Of course, the other important gift we had was imagination, and my imagination sometimes ran away with me. I still, to this day, remember having tea with the two youngest of my uncles, Malcolm and Ralph. There was no room for us around the dining table, so we had been relegated to the kitchen table to eat our meal. I, or someone, must have mentioned Wee Willy Winkle, the little man whose rhyme was told to children at bedtime, for I distinctly remember Ralph telling me he was going to kill him, and to this day, I can visualise a minute figure dressed in a long nightgown, a long tasselled cap on his head and holding a lantern walking across the table and then Ralph, brandishing a carving knife, swiping down at the figure. There was no horror, no blood, just an empty table and Wee Willy Winkle had disappeared forever!

Another story I recall was when Malcolm and Roy came home from church brandishing a lovely apple which was given to me. They told me it was magic and had been given to them by a fairy they had met in the woods around the big oak tree near the entrance. Of course, I spent endless visits to that oak tree, but never saw the fairy!

One of my final memories of life with my grandparents was the day when there was great excitement in the road as two or three of the households were fostering German children who were refugees from Nazi Germany. They were arriving at our small local railway station and not only the fostering families, but all the children in the road, decided to meet them. I remember us all walking to the station and the excitement whilst we waited for the train. I can vaguely remember one of the boys and I am not sure how long they stayed, but we tend to forget how many thousands of refugees were fleeing a ruined Germany.

It is only now, many, many years later that I realise that because my father was absent I 'adopted' all men as my father figure. Not once did I use the term 'grandpa', or any other usual affectionate term for one's grandfather. My maternal great-grandfather I called 'Daddy Bill', my maternal grandfather 'Dad Charlie', my paternal grandfather 'Dad Williams' and our next-door neighbour 'Daddy Garlick'. What a strange child was I!

CHAPTER 2

Schooldays

I knew the time was coming when I would have to start school and I wanted to go to Baglan School, where all my friends went (it has since become St. Baglan's Church). I was told that I could not, and I had to go to live in Aberavon with my parents and attend the Mountain School there. I was SO unhappy. Firstly, I wanted to stay in Baglan and secondly, I wanted to go to the small friendly school there.

The day came when I left, and I can distinctly remember how sad I was and even more sad when I saw where I was going to live. A small, terraced house, one amongst streets of houses and furthermore there was NO garden! Gone were the lawn, the apple trees, the chicken run; here you were enclosed by brick walls and a concrete floor. There were two bedrooms and mine was in the back, overlooking the lane behind and the yard next door. When I moved there my parents were in the process of having a bathroom built next to the kitchen. For a few weeks, until its completion, I had to bath in a zinc bath which was placed in front of the fire!

It is amazing to think how different life was in those days. Many people had no bathrooms; many only had outside toilets, usually located at the end of the garden; fridges were a rarity, as were washing machines; few people had telephones, and hardly anyone had a television. I can distinctly remember when my father bought our first television – we were the first in the street to own one. He bought it just in time for the Coronation of our present Queen, in June 1953. All televisions then were in black and white – no colour. The screens were tiny – ours had a twelve-inch screen, so my father bought a special 'magnifier' which was placed in front of the screen and tied on with large hessian type straps. It really was a different world.

The old lady who lived next door was Irish, incredibly old (or seemed so to me at that time!) and she always wore black with a woollen shawl (grey?) wrapped around her. She would take her stooped form out to the yard in the morning and there she would turn on the outside tap and wash in cold water, whatever the weather. She was always kind to me, and on St. Patrick's Day she would have fresh shamrocks sent over from Ireland, and I was always given some!

I'm not sure at what age I started school, but I assume it was just before my fifth birthday – or was it my sixth? My early memories of my move to Aberavon and starting school are not good. I hated living there and the unhappiness must have permeated through my body, resulting in nightmares and toilet accidents – not happy memories. Other memories, a little later, were of me collapsing with terrible pain when walking home from school. This happened several times, and each time someone would fetch my mother to get me home. The problem was appendicitis, and on February 14th, 1948, aged seven, I went into the local Aberavon hospital (long gone) and there my GP removed my appendix. Yes, in those days, GPs were often surgeons as well – quite different times! I can remember my mother and grandmother being there when I first opened my eyes after the operation. This was also a time when people had to pay to see the doctor and for operations, as the NHS did not come into being until July of that year. How much my operation cost I do not know.

My most vivid recollection of those early days in Aberavon was just after I had started school. Winter was approaching and my mother, at great expense, bought me a black Burberry coat –then extremely popular rainwear/outer wear for children. I was SO proud of my new coat. I used to go home for lunch, but a friend of mine – her name was Janet – lived on Baglan Road. Janet used to catch the bus which was just down the hill from the school. I REALLY wanted to show my new coat to my grandmother, so I decided I would get on the bus with Janet. Janet paid her money to the conductor (an old halfpenny) and asked for the Sarn Farn stop. I also had a halfpenny, so I gave it to the conductor and asked for Sunnycroft. He must have been a horrible man as he looked at me (a very small five-year-old) and said, 'that isn't enough, it's a penny to Sunnycroft, you'll have to get off at Sarn Farn'. So, along with Janet, I disembarked at Sarn Farn and there was Janet's Mum, waiting for her. On seeing me, and hearing what had happened, she waited with me for the next bus and gave me another halfpenny to get me to Sunnycroft.

In those days there were very few cars on the road, so after alighting from the bus I walked across the main road and up to my grandmother's house. I cannot remember which of the boys were there, but I seem to remember there were others eating at the table with my grandparents. My grandmother made a huge fuss of me, asked how I had got there etc and sat me down to eat. With that, I remember looking out of the window and seeing my father getting off his carrier bike (it had a carrier at the front in which he could put newspapers when he collected them from the station), As he came in – obviously angry because I had gone missing and caused much worry – I can vividly remember my gran shielding me and saying, 'Don't shout at her'. How I got back to school I do not remember, probably sitting in the carrier!

You have probably guessed that my father, Ron Williams, was a newsagent. He inherited the shop from his aunt, Elizabeth Tapp Jones, whom I called 'Bopa', which is Welsh for aunt. It was a small shop which sold, along with newspapers, all sorts of other things. On the outside of the counter were crates of lemonade, and other crates full of empty bottles ready to be returned to the supplier. In those days lemonade was always sold in bottles and children would go around the streets offering to take your bottles back to the shop as they then received money; it was only coppers, but it supplemented the children's pocket money. Alongside those were bundles of firewood, as the main form of heating in those days was a coal fire. On the opposite side was a stand selling cards for all occasions, and behind the counter were shelves filled with glass jars of every sweet you could think of – wonderful! Other shelves held a variety of items, from Reckitts' Blue to nibs for wooden pens and bars of red sealing wax. There were other items, too, kept for men who were calling in on their way to work at 6 am, bags of sugar and some tinned foods. People would pay into an 'Xmas Club' and order the Christmas annuals they wanted for their children, the Beano, The Dandy, Schoolfriend etc. Oh, so different from today!

One thing that always amused me was that in the 'storeroom' (which led from the shop) placed on a high shelf (I assume put there so that I could not reach them – they were stored 'secretly') were boxes of female necessities, sanitary towels. Rather than come in and use that word to my father (my mother was not always there), the women used to ask my father for a packet of 'thank gods'. With little contraception, they were relieved to find that they were not pregnant, so the arrival of a period was a time to say 'Thank god'!

My great aunt ('Bopa') always lived with my paternal grandparents, a very smart woman, and I had always wondered why she had never married. It was kept a big secret and it was many, many years before I learned the true, sad story of her life. Apparently, she had been married, to a man who drank, gambled, and enjoyed hitting his wife. She became pregnant and lost the baby when he threw her down the stairs. After that she threw him out. I believe she owned the house. He ended up in the Swansea workhouse, a place where the homeless and poor were often placed. Apparently, she visited him once or twice when he was there and when he died, she paid for his funeral. Such a sad, sad story. She must have been an exceptional woman for her time, as after being on her own she set up a business which my father later inherited.

I have not yet said much about my grandfather, Charles Murray. Although very 'Victorian' in some ways with strict discipline with the boys, male dominance etc, he was always gentle with me. Two things I wished I had done, which he tried to encourage in me but failed. One was to read music and play the piano, the other was to 'read' the stars. My grandfather had seen so many changes in his life. He had been christened a Roman Catholic – his father, Charles Murray, was of Irish descent and a Roman Catholic, his mother was Church of England. His father died at the age of 50 of a brain haemorrhage and therefore his mother had him confirmed in the Church of England. His Roman Catholic roots must have stood by him, as he never attended the same church as my grandmother, but preferred the high church of Margam Abbey, where he was a chorister for over 50 years. As a young man he had been at sea and told me the story of when he sailed to Chile and how dangerous it was under sail, going around the Cape. An intelligent man, he was also the Victorian epitome of males – his word was law and I remember how, when the radio was turned on for the news, no one was allowed to speak, and we all obeyed him. I still have the full set of Dickens books that he gave me.

Another memory of precious time spent with my grandparents was holidays. The only holidays I had as a child were with them, and they took me to their favourite places, either Paignton or Brixham in Devon. I used to be SO excited going and loved every minute. My grandfather bought me a toy boat I could sail on ponds. We went on boat trips, walked around harbours, and visited nearby places like the village of Cockington, Buckfast Abbey and Torquay. Unfortunately, I never had a holiday with my parents, though they went on a few cruises, leaving me with one of my uncles to look after me as by then my grandmother was no longer with us.

Sadly, my grandmother died, of cancer, when I was ten. She used to tell me that she was waiting to see me in my grammar school uniform, but unfortunately she never did. I vividly remember the day she died. It must have been a Friday, as every Friday I went to my paternal grandmother's house for lunch. I was walking back to school when a bus pulled up at the bus stop I was passing and out jumped one of my uncles, whose name was Malcolm (he was nine years older than I). I shouted out his name and he just looked back, did not smile, and merely said 'hallo, love'. I knew than that something was wrong.

I had visited my grandmother in hospital, and she was so weak she could hardly speak to me. In class that afternoon, one of the girls (who lived in my grandmother's road) shouted out 'your grandmother is dead'. I burst into tears, and the teacher, unable to comfort me, took me into the headmistress's room, where I cried and cried. Once settled and comforted, I returned to the classroom. Our school was on the top of a hill, and when we left, I was surprised when I walked to the bottom to see some neighbours of ours meeting me. They had their son (who was a year younger than I) with them and they told me they were taking me for tea and then to the September fair. I said nothing about my grandmother, and I can remember pretending that everything was all right, whilst inside I was hurting so much and feeling so sad. I must have acted very well, and at about 9 pm they took me home. Only then did my mother tell me the sad news, and only then could I give vent to my pain.

I eventually settled into school, but never really settled into living in the town. I continued to attend Baglan Church and was confirmed and married there. I am jumping ahead now, but I made friends and got used to school life. I cannot remember much about sitting the scholarship examination, but I passed, and I remember the headmistress, in morning assembly, asking me to stand up and then asking the school to clap as I had passed the arithmetic paper with flying colours, coming in as first in the borough! I was extremely excited and ran home that day. I knew my father was away on a newsagents' conference, so I went straight to our shop and told my mother 'I have passed'.

Sadly, my grandmother never had the pleasure of seeing me in the green uniform of the grammar school, now renamed Dyffryn Grammar. I suppose the school's claim to fame was that both Richard Burton and Anthony Hopkins were former pupils. The pass meant a school blazer – which I hated, as my mother bought it 'to allow for growth', so it was too big, but sadly I stopped growing, and the blazer always remained too large. Also, at great expense, I was given a nice leather satchel.

On to grammar school

Grammar school was an entirely new experience – much larger, much grander than anything I had previously experienced. Apart from the cookery, woodwork, and PE teachers, the teachers all strutted around in cloaks. I think they enjoyed the sense of theatre, especially when they strode around the yard which led from the lower to upper school and the wind would send their gowns billowing behind them, giving an illusory sense of grandeur. Later in life I became a teacher myself, and even though I recognised even then that some of the teaching left a lot to be desired, I am now appalled, when I look back, at how abysmally, in the main, we were taught.

We had a wonderful R.E. teacher, whom everyone loved, but we also laughed at him. The first introduction to R.E. was always the dance of the seven veils, when his rotund body and exaggerated speech would imitate the dance movements and accompany them with the story.

Maths: how on earth can a girl who passed arithmetic top of the borough then fail GCSE maths? Basically, dreadful teaching!

Similarly, how can someone who loved reading and loved history become bored and uninterested in the subject? Our history teacher (who regularly had a liquid lunch at the nearby Conservative club) only ever entered the classroom, shouted 'turn to page X and copy it'. On looking back, I am appalled and saddened that so much pleasure and interest were destroyed in this way.

English – our teacher was a man who had distinct favourites and if you were not one of them, he paid you little attention.

Our art teacher was a superb artist and an excellent teacher, but he had a violent temper and was prone to hitting boys over the head. I can remember him on one occasion throwing a boy down the stone stairs that led to the art room.

I am painting a very bleak picture, but it was of its time, and I also have many, many happy memories. I am also sad that my laziness and complacency did not make me work harder, and my foolish pride did not allow me to stay on and take my 'A' levels.

Of course, your parents' educational achievement gives you a huge educational advantage or disadvantage depending on their interest and encouragement. Sadly, my father had little education, and my mother, although intelligent, had to focus on assisting in the care of her siblings. I can never remember any books at home, apart from a library novel which my mother sometimes read.

My favourite subjects were English literature and foreign languages, I started studying Latin, but decided I would not continue with it in Form 3. I can remember the teacher sending for my mother and telling her that I was a natural linguist and should continue with Latin. Of course, my mother never even tried to dissuade me from dropping the subject, a decision which I regret to this day.

In Form 3 I took French and Spanish, both of which I loved and did extremely well in. I adored my language teacher, who gave me every encouragement. Sadly, it was my disappointment in my 'O' level results in these subjects that made me leave school. Being honest, it was probably a lot to do with deflated pride. My favourite language was Spanish, and in each exam I came top. In those days, a lecturer from London University used to come to conduct the oral examination. Before the Spanish oral, my teacher rehearsed with me and said that if he asked what I was hoping to do after university I was to say that I was keen to study French and Spanish at the Sorbonne in Paris. Imagine my delight when, just as I was about to leave school on the afternoon of the oral examination, my language teacher came running after me and said, looking extremely happy, 'Helena, he has given you 98%'.

One of my Spanish class, a boy whom I shall not name, was hopeless in the subject and would typically get between 12 and 20 marks in his Spanish exam. Can you imagine my dismay and horror when the 'O' level results were published (in those days they were put in the local newspaper, for all to see) and I had failed Spanish, whereas this boy, incredibly, had passed? I begged my mother to ask for my paper to be remarked, but all that happened was that the head rang the examining board and confirmed that I had failed. There was no visual examination of my paper and the case was closed.

I did not work for my exams and passed English, both Literature and Grammar, Religion, and French. Through laziness (I was sunbathing on the beach) I did not revise for the architecture exam, so I passed both art papers but failed architecture (in those days you had to pass all three papers) and therefore did not pass Art! Failing Spanish just broke my heart and I stupidly decided to leave school.

Rules in grammar school were quite strict, and one of these was that you adhered strictly to the school uniform. We girls (until Sixth Form) had to wear a white shirt, the green/black striped school tie, green blazer (with school badge) and a hideous green beret, which we all hated. Our gym slips were shapeless black garments consisting of three wide box pleats and tied in the middle with a narrow green sash. They were completely shapeless, and I often wonder if they were so designed to hide the developing bodies of young girls. Shapeless or not, we were still able to attract the opposite sex and I distinctly remember my first beau, a lovely chap two years my senior, waiting for me at the school gate and carrying my satchel home for me. Oh, the days of chivalry!

At the end of the day, as soon as we were a fair distance from the school on our homeward trek, we would feel safe enough to take off the hideous berets and stuff them into our pockets. We did not bargain for the fact that some of the staff (especially the senior mistress, Miss Thorn) might pass us in their homeward bus. Then, in the assembly the next day, we would be singled out and usually given a lecture and a week's detention!

A first taste of travel

It was whilst I was in grammar school that I had my first taste of travel. I went on two school trips abroad. The first, when I was fourteen, was to France, and it was on this trip that I became friends with a group of girls one year senior to me; we have remained friends ever since. Of course Britain, at that time, had only recently come out of rationing, which ended in 1954. Our clothes were plain and simple, our food much the same. To this day I can remember the wonderful smells emanating from those lovely old French village houses, the smell of frites being cooked in olive oil, the wafts of garlic, the wonderful baguettes, but most of all, coloured ice cream and even more astonishing, coloured shoes! It was a wonderful experience, but one which I think most young people today would not want. We slept in dormitories in French schools and were strictly watched over by the French/Spanish teacher and the senior mistress (who also taught French). Associating with the opposite sex was frowned upon, though there were one or two escapades!

Both the accommodation and food were basic, to say the least, and we were treated almost like prisoners. The journey began with a train journey to Dover, then the crossing to Paris. How I loved Sacré Coeur – the building itself, but also the approach. All those steps, all those artists. The atmosphere was magical. We visited there and Notre Dame and then Miss Thorn (senior mistress) announced that we should visit the Louvre. We were on the other side of Paris, so getting to the Louvre on a hot July day necessitated a long and arduous walk across Paris. This we did, only to find the Louvre closed on that day, so the visit was abandoned and unfortunately, we never got to go back.

From Paris we journeyed across France to Bayonne, a long, tiring trek on post-war trains which then only had wooden slatted seats. It was still a magical introduction into a world outside Britain, and I still remember being at the harbour in St. Jean de Luz and watching the firework display on Bastille night, it was a wonderful experience.

A year or two later I went on another school holiday, this time to Switzerland. Again, it was a great experience, but nothing to compare with that first trip to France. Perhaps it was France itself, or perhaps it was because it was so close to the end of the war.

Teenage life

I remained friends with the group of people I had mixed with on that French sojourn. We had great times together, boys and girls. In summer we would meet at the beach and sometimes had a barbecue. Otherwise, we would stroll around the local park, sometimes have a game of tennis, and sometimes we would watch the boys play soccer. I distinctly remember one girl who really was not part of our usual group organising a party at her aunt's flat (the aunt was away). We were excited and felt quite wicked – a mixed group without an adult in sight! Today you would be talking about people going to bed; for us, nothing so adult and daring. We thought WE were daring, the boys sitting, and the girls moving from lap to lap and kissing each one! Oh dear, despite being teenagers, we were extremely innocent and naive!

These were also the days of rock and roll, Bill Haley, the Platters and crooners like Frank Sinatra, Bing Crosby etc. The days when boys came over to a girl and asked if she would dance with him, the days of narrow waists, hooped skirts and frilled undergarments. The days when, if a boy liked you and he saw you dancing with someone else, he would walk over, tap whoever your dancing partner was, on the shoulder, and then take you in his arms. girls always liked this, it showed you were attractive, and you could then proudly say that you were 'tagged'. It was the time when teenagers danced all night, usually either in a church hall or in the YMCA as we got older, and we travelled to the Porthcawl Pavilion, which was perceived as being more 'sophisticated'. I remember dancing to the wonderful 'big band' sound of someone called Harry Mattock in the YMCA. Looking back, I realise how lucky we were, in many respects.

The other big attraction was the cinema, and on Saturday evenings there would be awfully long queues to get in. If you had a date you would probably sit in the back row and wait nervously until his arm went around, you and then there would be the kisses! There was one small cinema, in a place called Taibach, and a crowd of us (boys and girls) all went there to see the film *Bill Haley and Rock Around The Clock*. Oh, how daring were we, standing up and jiving in the aisles! Yes, those were the tender days of rock and roll, jiving, the occasional under-age glass of alcohol, the start of sexual activity, which stopped at a little petting, and if you did that you felt guilty!

It was also a time when religion was important in most families and a Sunday evening would see us all (after church/chapel), girls dressed in their Sunday best and boys in their suits, walking in the town and then meeting in the local café for a coffee.

I distinctly remember seeing, or rather noticing, my husband-to-be for the first time. I was about 15 years of age, upstairs in the grammar school (where the languages room was). We girls decided to look down and 'view' the 'old boys' rugby team who were visiting the school and I saw this chap with red hair, kneeling to tie his laces on his rugby boots, and thought 'he looks nice'. That was the start. He asked me out the following week and we became an item. The courtship ended when he was posted (as part of his compulsory National Service) to Iraq for a year, between 1957-58. Whilst there he witnessed the revolution which resulted, on July 14th 1958, in the overthrow of the then king -Faisal II and the end of the monarchy in that country. John was based at Habbaniya and as a wireless operator (he never forgot the morse code) he was one of the first to monitor the Russian launching of the famous "Sputnik". On his return, our friendship continued and remained, despite us being geographically apart for two years (John was at St. Luke's College, Exeter).

We would marry on Boxing Day 1960, three months after he had started teaching.

CHAPTER 3

Early years of marriage

How different things were regarding contact when I was a teenager in the 1950s! No internet, no mobiles and few people even had telephones. I used to wait for the postman to bring those lovely letters from John – how I wish I had kept some of them. On a Sunday evening I would unlock my father's newsagent's shop (which had a telephone) and wait for John to call at the pre-arranged time for our weekly conversation.

But I am speeding ahead. During these years, and after my 'O' level disappointment, I had left school – despite my language teacher's pleas, I had gone to work in Lloyds Bank. I enjoyed my time there but left a few months before my marriage for another post which offered more money, an asset we had little of.

Looking back, I do have regrets: I regret that I did not sit my 'A' levels and go on to university; I regret that we married so young. Of the latter, I do not regret marrying my husband, but we were both too young. The reason for this was of its time: little contraception, no pill etc. I was terrified in case the temptation was so great that I would become pregnant, and I knew how horrified my parents would have been. In those days, especially in Wales, pregnancy before marriage was a thing of shame, now I think how stupid, narrow and harmful those attitudes were.

Thirteen months after our marriage our son Nigel was born and in giving birth I almost lost my life. He was transverse, and even after I had been in hospital for three weeks prior to his arrival, a caesarean section was not performed. Eventually, after hours and hours in the final stage of labour, I had a massive haemorrhage, and only then did the doctors arrive, anaesthetise me, and deliver him with high forceps. Of course, in those days, husbands were not allowed anywhere near the delivery room.

The next morning, I can remember awakening, still in the labour ward, and realising that the birth had occurred. I saw a nurse pass the open door and called out 'Nurse, what have I had?' (it did not occur to me that the baby could have died). She answered, 'a boy, I'll bring him'. On entering the room carrying Nigel, her first words were 'you realise you both almost died, don't you?' Of course, I did not.

I could see Nigel, but not to hold him, and I was then not allowed to see him, apart from visiting him in his cot, for the following three days. Many months later, I discovered that they thought he would be brain damaged, but thankfully this never happened, and he was our much-loved son. The experience was not pleasant, and I remember years later in Kenya, when my doctor, Lady Boyd, read my notes, she passed the remark 'they should have been horse-whipped!' Despite this I desperately wanted another child, mainly because I hated being an only child and wanted mine to have a sibling. I was told that because of the problems following the birth I would be unable to conceive, but conceive I did, and we were blessed with a beautiful daughter, Sue.

Those early years were not easy; our finances were dire. John was earning £9 a week, whilst the apprentices he was teaching were earning £12 a week! After our marriage we had lived with my parents, using their study as our separate living room. When Nigel was six months old my mother decided she wanted to move and got my father to do the dirty work, ie, asking us to find elsewhere to live. Although saving hard, we did not have a deposit for a house, so my mother-in-law told us of a gentleman who lived in a large house in Port Talbot and was prepared to give free accommodation in return for doing the housework, cooking and laundry. We would have to pay half the heating/electricity bills.

Memories of the months we spent there are still like a nightmare. The man was elderly, selfish and a miser. I was virtually an unappreciated slave and after six months we happily moved into our first home of our own. It was not where we wanted to live, but we managed to get a mortgage and as we did not own a car, John had to walk to the college where he was lecturing. We decorated, putting up nursery wallpaper and lemon curtains in Nigel's room, and a new fireplace in the lounge. We were so poor we could not even afford carpets, but my father took me to a carpet sale in Cardiff where he bought us enough carpet to put downstairs. I always remember it was paper thin and a black/white mottled design, but better that concrete floors, and we were so grateful to my father. My father's aunt bought us stair carpet, my grandfather gave us his old lounge furniture and we were in heaven!

We had only lived there for about one year when my father

told us of a builder friend of his who was building new properties in Baglan. Obviously Baglan was, at that time, my favourite place, and after seeing the plans of the house and obtaining an increased mortgage we moved into a home where we went on to live for many years and were extremely happy. It was here that Sue was conceived, and both the children had many friends and much happiness here.

Thoughts of our years there are an integral and important part of my life, and probably some of my happiest years. We were not rich, but we were so happy, John using his woodworking expertise made bookshelves and coffee tables for the lounge (I remember the wood being Parana pine). As was the fashion then, he used pine to clad the kitchen walls and we thought we were SO modern! He still worked three nights a week taking a night class, as we needed every penny to pay the mortgage.

They were happy years for the children, as the road consisted mostly of young families, so there was no shortage of friends for our two. It was a time of 'community' when we all helped each other and looked out for each other and our children.

July brought the annual Baglan carnival, and one year we thought it would be a good idea if our road entered the float competition. A float was a long lorry, on the trailer of which would be a themed display. The first one we decided on (after a communal meeting) was to take the title of Walt Disney's 'Jungle Book'. John offered to paint the backdrop and after it was decided what characters the children were, as individuals, to depict, the mothers had the task of making the costumes.

Nigel was elected to play the part of Shere Khan. I made his outfit out of mustard-coloured cotton and spent ages cutting 'stripes' out of black sticky tape and fitting them on the suit. John and I combined efforts in the mask for his head and he looked almost authentic!

Sue had a brown woolly outfit, as she was one of the monkeys. John made the 'flat' –a wooden background – and propped it up under our carport where he painted a lovely jungle scene with a cascading waterfall in the centre. As soon as he started painting the children in the road would stand around him, watching as the 'jungle' became reality.

The big day came, and the children, resplendent in their outfits, music from the film accompanying them, and enjoying waving to the throngs of Baglan residents who had turned out to watch, loved every minute. The climax of the day was winning the competition and being awarded the silver cup! There was a great deal of celebration in the road that night, firstly a children's' party and later the adults.

We went on to compete over the next few years, one theme being Treasure Island and the next depicting the deep south of America. We won each time, and eventually were asked, politely, not to compete the following year to allow others the chance of winning!

What happy, happy memories. We may have been quite poor, but you cannot buy happiness.

A job in Uganda

It was during this time that we started talking about working abroad. There were always teaching posts advertised for the developing countries, and John and I both wanted to travel in a way that would allow us to have some money in the bank. In 1967 he applied through the Ministry of Overseas Development for a teaching post in Uganda. We were delighted when he was accepted, and I was beside myself with excitement. Then the unexpected happened: John was called into the Principal's office and offered promotion. This obviously meant a pay rise, and a was a step in the right direction career wise. John accepted, and the Principal then said 'well, I don't now need to fill in this report for the MOD, do I?' (Ministry of Overseas Development). I was bitterly disappointed, but my husband pointed out that once he had this promotion it would remain, and he could then apply for an overseas posting the following year. This he did, and that was the start of my love of Africa. In August 1968 we flew to Kenya with our two children, Nigel, aged six, and Sue, aged three.

On 31st July that year I had been in hospital having a hysterectomy (the aftereffects of Nigel's birth had left irreparable damage to the womb), and in those days this was major surgery and involved a two-week stay in hospital. This was also my first clash with cancer; they also removed my cervix as apparently there were cancerous cells. I often thought how lucky I was – without the surgery, the cancer might have progressed.

We had moved out of our house prior to my hospital stay and had let it furnished to a nice young couple, and we stayed with my parents until we were flying to Kenya. We were SO excited, and I smile now when I think of how we dressed to take the flight to Africa. All very formal, John and Nigel in suits, me in a dress and matching coat (I think I also had gloves) and Sue had a dress and coat. My outfit, and Sue's coat, were made of a then 'amazing' new material called Crimplene.

In those days flying was a huge adventure, and people thought I was mad going to Africa with two young children. Going abroad at that time was a novelty, but it was just the start of people taking holidays abroad, Spain and France being the most popular destinations. Members of the family came to the station to bid farewell, perhaps thinking they would never see us again!

We caught the train to London and then on to Heathrow to take our flight with BOAC. I loved the feeling of that plane travelling down the runway and then surging up into the sky –

I still think that is the nicest part of a flight.

Kenya, 1968-1970

The plane was full of young families, all going to Kenya and employed by the Ministry of Overseas Development. There were many babies on board, accommodated in mesh 'hammocks' which hung above the seats. We comprised a mixture of qualifications and careers, some teachers, some vets, some agronomists etc, but one thing we shared was that we were all young and enthusiastic. I seem to remember us stopping on the Continent – it may have been Italy – for refuelling, and then we went on until we reached Entebbe in Uganda. Here we were to disembark and in the airport building (which was extremely basic) there was a beautiful buffet breakfast laid out for us. Sadly, just as we were descending for Entebbe, Nigel started to be violently sick and consequently ate hardly anything of the prepared feast.

We then re-embarked for the final part of our journey, landing in Nairobi the day after we had left London. The cries of babies and the crowded plane meant that none of us slept much on the flight, and I was particularly exhausted when we reached our destination. I had not completely recovered from surgery, and was not in the best of health, having a huge dressing on to cover the two stitch abscesses I had.

We were taken to an hotel called Brunners. Last time I was in Nairobi I looked for it, but it must have disappeared many years ago. It was situated just off Government Road and we were given an upstairs room which had a balcony overlooking the road outside. That sounds very grand, but believe me, it was a very basic hotel.

John was told he had to go to Government House, along with all the other teachers, to fill in all the necessary paperwork (the Africans loved paperwork) and to be given an introductory talk. When he had left, I settled Sue into the cot-type bed she had, and Nigel lay on a small single bed. I lay down and all three of us fell fast asleep. The next thing I remember is being shaken awake by one of the staff (of course, being half-asleep, I thought this man was going to attack me). An extremely nice Kenyan, he then explained that my daughter had screamed loudly, and he had come in to check that she was all right. Nigel and I were both so exhausted we had slept through Sue's screams, and believe me, she had powerful lungs!

That evening we all went for a walk. It was my mother's birthday in September, and I bought her a silver brooch which we then posted to the UK. On returning to our hotel, we heard a great deal of noise on the road outside, so we went on to the balcony and there witnessed a European driver being shot and killed by an African. What a start to our Kenyan life!

The next day we had to walk to a certain spot where we were picked up by a Peugeot 'taxi' (commonly called matatus). These estate cars were widely used for what was called the 'death run', from Nairobi to up country to Nakuru first, then Eldoret and finally Kitale. Eldoret was 193 miles from Nairobi, so we were looking at a six or seven-hour journey. Every seat was taken in the estate car, so it was not to be a luxurious, or even a comfortable journey.

The drive was spectacular, if a little hair raising, as the driver did not slow down at bends and at times I thought we were going to end up in the Rift itself! The escarpment climb was wonderful, and as we left Nairobi we saw, for the first time, local vendors selling their wares at the roadside, everything from fruit and vegetables to woven plates and wooden carvings. We did not stop, of course, as the driver was merely delivering us to our destination, Eldoret.

Up and up we climbed, with many dangerous bends. We eventually reached our approximate halfway stop, Nakuru. Later I found Nakuru a pleasant town with an excellent hotel called the Stags Head (we loved the Sunday buffet there). It had been founded by the famous – or infamous – Lord Delamere. Our driver, however, did not show us the nice side of Nakuru, but the run-down area with garages and a few 'dukas' (shops) where we could buy a can of cold drink. By this time both Sue and I were desperate for a toilet – I am not sure where John took Nigel, but I went into one of these dukas and asked the proprietor, and Indian gentleman, if he knew of a toilet where I could take my daughter. He looked at us closely, as if deciding if we could be trusted, and then ceremoniously took a key out of a tin box. This, he explained, was the key to his private toilet. He directed us to the outside back garden and pointed to a shack at the bottom. Feeling greatly honoured, I took Sue and unlocked the door, expecting to find a clean white porcelain toilet, but behold, there was nothing but a long drop! Sue then became deliberately stubborn, not wanting to use this facility, but when

I carefully lifted her and held her legs astride she was able to relieve herself, and I followed suit!

After this short break we continued our journey up through the escarpment, climbing ever higher and around many hair-raising bends, We passed through Timboroa, the highest spot in the Highlands, and I remember everything looking so green and verdant. I knew extraordinarily little about Africa, and certainly not Kenya, before living there and my perception from school-days was that Africa was dry and arid. How untrue! Here were green fields and thick forests. Many women were selling fruit and potatoes alongside the road and there were fields of beautiful pyrethrums.

We were now entering the Uasin Gishu plateau, which was to be our home for the next two years. Timboroa was the highest point of the Kenyan highlands, being 9557 ft above sea level. Situated on the equator, people (including ourselves) used to stop here and have photos taken with one leg in the northern emisphere and one in the southern!

No stop for us on this occasion, as our driver was all too anxious to conclude the journey. On we drove, the countryside lush with thick forests of blue gum trees, and then we finally approached Eldoret. We were dropped off in the centre of the town and greeted by one of the lecturers, named Alf, from the Rift Valley Technical College, where my husband was to teach English to the students. He explained that the Principal, a Mr Bridges, had asked him to collect us and take us to the college. Alf also told us that we were highly honoured as Bridges did not normally look after newcomers, and Alf believed that we were to spend our first night in the Eldoret Golf Club.

I am jumping ahead. First we were taken to the Principal's house, a bungalow in the grounds of the college. We were greeted by his wife (I was told that she was a white Russian), who was an attractive and charming lady. She gave us afternoon tea and then the Principal took us to our first night's abode, a rondavel (circular thatched building) in the grounds of the golf club. Exhausted, we got the children showered and into bed and soon followed ourselves. I can distinctly remember awakening during the night and being afraid that some animal was going to enter the room – it was merely the colobus monkeys jumping on the roof!

Hill School

The next day we were taken to the Hill School. This was a beautiful school which sadly was not as much used as it had been in the past, as since 'Uhuru', the day when Kenya became independent (13/12/1963), many white settlers had left Kenya, either to go to South Africa, UK, Australia or elsewhere, feeling that they would not be able to survive under Black rule. Still beautiful with its long white buildings, terracotta roofs and well-manicured grounds, it was an impressive sight.

We were introduced to a couple who taught at the school who had a young daughter named Rebecca—we later became firm friends. This was the school Nigel was to attend, and it was where we were given a small upstairs flat in which to spend our first months. 'Small' was the operative word. It had a tiny, poorly equipped kitchen (more like a galley), a small living area and one bedroom. Outside our bedroom was a door which led to the long corridor with dormitories leading off it. As there was only one bedroom in the flat, we left this door open and the children slept in the first dormitory which had, if I remember correctly, about eight beds. The whole place was filthy, with cobwebs, dust, and we later discovered rats, which we managed to eliminate.

We were introduced to the headmistress – a formidable lady named Jane Barbour, one of an old Kenyan farming family from the Kitale area who were heavily involved with car racing and the East African Safari. They were also great rugby enthusiasts and my husband later became friendly with one of them, I think his name was George. I distinctly remember a later date when he called to our house and asked John to go for a spin in his rally car, and the 'spin' became a 200-mile round trip to Nakuru and back, with a few beers in between!

We were truly blessed to have been given a posting in such a beautiful place. Eldoret then was small, compact, friendly. (Then, circa 18,000 people – in 2019 it was almost 476,000). Its European origins were from the Boers who had come to Kenya in search of a new life, back at the beginning of the 20th century. Very hardy people, they had trekked, with their ox carts laden with all their belongings, from Mombasa, where they had landed, and continued through to Nairobi and then on, upwards through the escarpment until they reached the Uasin Gishu plateau. There are many stories as to why they settled here, the obvious one being the verdant countryside and the altitude, which was conducive to farming. The other, more outrageous story is that one of the ox carts collapsed under the weight of an extraordinarily strong metal safe, and the owner then decided that he would build a bank around the safe, hence the origins of the Standard Bank, Eldoret!

In those days Kenya was divided into 'plots', many made available to soldiers who had fought in the First World War.

Apparently Eldoret was Plot 64 – I remember my husband having a tie with '64' printed all over it. The name 'Eldoret' was given by the Governor and originated with the Masai word 'Eldare', which meant 'hard rocks' – a reference to the stony bed of the Sosiani river which ran through the town. The then Governor added the letter 't' to the end, thus making 'Eldaret'. When, however, the name was announced in print, there was a printing error which was never rectified and Eldaret became the Eldoret of today.

The Eldoret I remember was reminiscent of a town in the Wild West. Some shops even had a sort of balcony in front with a wooden post which looked as if it was meant for tethering your horse. There was a Post Office (built by an Afrikaner called Van Aardt, who built it when his attempt at farming failed); two hotels, the Lincoln and the central Wagon Wheel, a wonderful Goan tailor (whose name I cannot remember), Dot Hopper's coffee shop and bar, Hassanali's supermarket, Shah the camera shop (infamously called Shah the shark) and several garages. I remember being in town one day and everyone ended up hiding behind cars, as some criminals who apparently had come from Uganda had decided to break into the Standard Bank and were enjoying firing their guns wherever their fancy took them. I was told that the manager, a Scottish gentleman by the name of Morrison-Brown, infamously hid behind his desk with the wastepaper bin over his head! I also remember the beautiful Jacaranda trees which lined the High Street – when they were in bloom it was a sight to behold.

The Highlands had been a centre for the education of Europeans, probably because of its temperate climate, and the town had three incredibly good European standard schools – indeed, they were more in the manner of British public schools. They were the Hill School, where we initially lived, and where our son Nigel became a pupil, the Highlands school which was for girls, and the Loreto Convent, which again was predominantly female. How different school life was then. In the Hill School uniform was strict, and Nigel was kitted out with his grey shorts, blazer, tie, and trilby hat. For a while, I took the job (at £1 a day) of supervising the school lunches. Grace was always said, table manners adhered to and after lunch all pupils retired to a nearby dormitory where they had to lie down and rest for an hour. There was also, on a Friday morning, the weekly flag raising ceremony, where we all sang the National Anthem in Swahili, whilst the flag was raised. I must say that good manners were paramount, and Nigel soon got into the habit of standing up if a woman came into the room. If you were walking across the school grounds and some children were about (usually walking in crocodile style) the boys would immediately doff their trilby hats as a sign of respect!

Of course, although Nigel could start school, Sue was too young. I heard of a good nursery school, which I took her to, but as children are prone to doing, she started to cry when I left. 'Oh, she'll be fine' I was told. Not my daughter! When I collected her three hours later, she was still having occasional sobs and her face was swollen, with red, puffed, and tearful eyes! Not surprisingly, she never went again. We settled into our life and made the tiny flat as pleasant as possible. We became friends with Malcolm and Grace Nichols, who were our neighbours (but in a nice bungalow) and both taught at the Hill School. Malcolm was a keen member of the Uasin Gishu Arts Society and had produced several plays for the drama group. He persuaded me to join and so, leaving John in charge of the children, I went along to firstly the audition and later rehearsals at the lovely Uasin Gishu theatre. It was there that I took the lead in 'My Three Angels' in November,1968, playing the role of Emily Dulay.

Joining the theatre group meant meeting people and making friends, two of whom became close friends, a Kenyan (British) farmer named Dave Tooley who had married a lovely Canadian woman named Mary. Sadly, Mary died not long after giving birth to her daughter just after we had left Kenya. Also in the group was Mike Henson, a young agronomist, and he and his wife Nicola also became our friends.

Just after this we were told that the small bungalow on the College grounds (semi-detached) that should have been ready for us when we arrived was now completed and we could move in at the beginning of December. Great excitement and happiness. Yes, it was tiny, all rooms being small, but it had a veranda and a garden and was not reached by a flight of stairs. Also, it meant that John could walk into work as we were on the College campus and I had the use of the car to take Nigel into school, shop, etc. Our European neighbours were the Kellys, who had two children, and an Australian family named Hill who had four children, but one of them returned to Australia. Our children now had friends close by, which made life very pleasant.

We had taken on a house servant, the wonderful Charles, so I did not have any housework to do. We were desperately short of money (teachers were referred to as 'the poor whites of Africa') and I was bored and wanted to work anyway. Although not a qualified teacher I was offered a post as a nursery teacher at the Aga Khan Nursery School. Even by African standards, I was paid a pittance, earning the princely sum of £1 Kenyan pound for each half day.

Although not trained, I adapted and enjoyed the work. I made flash cards for reading, ordered some more 'modern' children's books, encouraged learning through play etc. The first day I explained to Sue, 'Mummy is going to work so that we have more money, but I will be home for lunch'. Charles was going to look after her (she and Charles got on very well). I should have known that this miniature of me was not going to be happy. When I returned at lunchtime there was a tear-stained little girl looking through the bedroom window who managed to make me feel I was the worst mother in the world! From that day on Sue came into the school with me and loved it.

One of my strongest memories of that time was of a little Asian boy called Ruknuddin. He hated school, would not play with the other children, and kept running off and hiding under a table. I soon realised that the poor child had the most awful stammer. I had taught speech/elocution to children in the UK and realised that Ruknuddin desperately needed help. On speaking to the boy's mother, I was told that he had acquired the stammer 'through eating too many sweets and ice cream'. I knew that this was nonsense and I also knew that he was not going to get the help he desperately needed and deserved. From then on, I took Ruknuddin each break-time and after his lunch and did various exercises inbreathing etc, and miraculously he improved. It was amazing to see the change in him and he started mixing with the others etc. A highly intelligent boy, I often wonder what became of him.

Our house servant – Charles

I cannot continue without mentioning Charles, who became one of the family. He had obviously worked for some of the old Colonials and seemed terribly 'respectful'. I was rather taken aback when, on the first day of his employment, he asked for a uniform. 'Sorry, Charles, I said, I only supply aprons'. (These were made from the wonderful Jinja cotton, which came in various colours and was used, in profusion, to change shabby, austere government furniture etc into colourful, attractive, and modern fittings.) Looking rather dismayed, Charles had to accept the situation.

After finishing work on the first day, he entered the lounge, turned towards John, saluted, and said 'Kwaheri, Bwana'. He then turned to me and repeated the process, replacing 'Bwana' with 'Memsahib'. John and I were both horrified, and I told Charles that he was NEVER to bow to us, and never SALUTE us – all we wanted was for him to shout 'kwaheri' (goodbye) as he left.

Of course, we were there only five years after Independence, and many of the old colonial rituals and habits remained – and I must say, many of the Africans seemed to prefer the 'old' ways, demeaning to the Africans as they were.

Charles settled in, and he was a gem. When an African came around selling live chickens, Charles would come and tell me, simultaneously advising me how many to buy and how much to pay. He would then feed and look after the chickens (they roamed in our back garden). When he felt one was ripe for killing, he would approach me and say 'Memsahib, kitchen tonight?' Yes, he could never say chicken – it was always a 'kitchen'.

He adored Sue, and vice versa. When he was cooking in the kitchen, he would lift her on to the work surface and dance and sing to her; she would help him lay the table for dinner, the two of them turning it into a tribal occasion with melodious chanting and pulsating movements. I remember on one occasion when Charles had baby sat for us to go out, we returned to find him not in the lounge, but sitting on the floor outside her bedroom. She had an upset stomach and had been sick, and Charles was guarding her closely. A good-looking man – I would say he was in his late 30s, possible early 40s – he had a wife and family some distance away. However, I would regularly see him, on a late Saturday afternoon, cycle into our drive with a lovely looking young African lady perched on his crossbar. The two would disappear into his accommodation and Charles would appear on Monday, alone as usual!

We decided to start Sue in the Loreto Convent, but this was later, when she reached four. She was SO happy there! She was tiny for four years old, and I can remember her first day, when all the older girls crowded around her, saying how sweet she was. Some Afrikaner farmer friends of ours, the Steenkamps, had two daughters in the school and as they knew Sue, they virtually adopted her. I will never forget her wonderful teacher, Sister Irene, who was in tears on the day Sue left, and who corresponded with Sue until she was very old and almost blind. Many years later, she died at Loreto, Mombasa.

Cats, dogs and parrots

It was whilst we lived in this small bungalow that we acquired our first pets: a lovely tabby cat which the children named 'Fluffy' and later a half-ridgeback mongrel who was christened 'Tramp' as he had been found and had no abode. He was a lovely puppy who was full of life and I can remember having great difficulty in trying to catch him for his first bath.

Later, we acquired a beautiful African Grey baby parrot. Sadly, Africans were prone to stealing young parrots from the nest to sell them. It was completely wrong, of course, and perhaps we should not have bought one, but what would have happened to them if they were unsold? As parrots have a reputation of being able to be quite nasty, we called this parrot 'Kali', though she was the most lovable, docile parrot. The poor young bird would not eat conventional parrot food and after taking advice, I prepared a mixture of hard-boiled egg and fine meal. This Kali would eat, but only from my hand. I believe that this is where we bonded, and she was a delightful pet. She was so tame that she rarely sat in her cage – only if she were outside on the veranda, or if Charles came into the room, for then she would squawk very loudly and sound ferocious. I often wondered if this was because Charles was black, and she had been stolen by Africans. If John was marking papers or preparing lessons on the dining room table she would fly over, stop, and then fix her beak around his pen whilst trying to drag it off him; when the children were eating their breakfast in the morning she would, again, land on the table, fix her beak around the edge of their cereal bowls and try to drag them away. She also developed a love of porridge! In the evenings, she would perch on my shoulder whilst I was reading or watching television and when asked, I could always get a kiss.

Then there were the ubiquitous chameleons, which terrified Charles and sadly, whenever he had the chance Nigel would take his chameleon close to him, and poor Charles would run off, terrified. After a severe reprimand, Nigel stopped this behaviour. I was given an explanation as to why Africans are afraid of chameleons, and whether it is true or not, I know that Charles certainly did not want to be near them. The story or fable goes like this:

When God made the world, all humans were black skinned, but God then created a huge lake and sent animals to the different countries to direct them to the lake where they could bathe and become white. To the UK he sent a cheetah, to other European countries other fast-running animals. By the time he got to Africa, God only had the chameleon, which he sent to direct the Africans. The chameleon, being so slow, got the Africans to the lake after the rest of the world and they found most of the water gone. Desperate, the Africans stood in the sparse water and rested their hands in it – which explains why the Africans have pale skin on the soles of their feet and palms of their hands!

As to whether this is a fable that Charles believed, I do not know, but I was acutely aware that he was extremely superstitious. Sadly, this story also illustrates the very wrong idea that being white was better than being black, which, as we all know, is completely untrue.

One of the students was an albino and I can assure you that it is distressing to see an African albino, as they stand out so much from their friends. This boy was almost blind, and had to be led by a friend around the campus. We and our European neighbours later bought him spectacles, which slightly helped, but at this stage he could see hardly anything. I was on the veranda and when Charles came outside, I pointed to the boy and said how sorry I was for him. Charles immediately said 'mbaya sana' (very bad) and told me that the boy was an albino because he was of mixed-race parentage. Try as I might, I could not convince him that this was not the case.

Other 'pets' were an injured owl, which Nigel was nursing back to health. Sadly, Sue left the bedroom door open, and the poor owl was devoured by Fluffy the cat! There was a honey badger for whom John had made a cage and run, but sadly we awoke one day to find it damaged and the badger gone.

Thinking of those two years spent in Kenya makes me SO happy. They were the happiest years of my life! So many lovely people, such a beautiful country. John played for the rugby team and we would give support for both home and away matches. I remember one occasion when the match was at Iten, a town which was at a higher altitude than Eldoret, 2,400m. John, playing on the wing, raced up the field and then blacked out. I ran down from the stand and was afraid he was dead, but he had fainted from the altitude! He recovered, but did not play in the rest of the game.

There were many rugby teams in Kenya – one was called the 'Nandi Bears', so called because of an old story about some wild animal rampaging the area which was never identified but referred to as the 'Nandi Bear'. A good rugby player was Scatty Meintjies, a really hard, tough, Afrikaner. I don't think the opposition had much chance if he tackled them! He also had quite a temper, but was always calmed by his lovely wife, Olga. We knew some lovely, hospitable Afrikaans families – all farmers. They were all so friendly and generous and we were often invited for sumptuous lunches or dinners. I remember Franz and Arkie Cloete; they had an enormous farm and what seemed like different parts of the house built in rondavels. Then there were Kurt and Anna Barnard, whose doors were always open, and I remember having dinner, then a party there and breakfast being served in the morning. We spent many happy hours with our friends the Tooleys, where the children would feed the lambs or calves and ride on ponies. The peacocks would be strolling on the lush lawns whilst Dave, John and the dogs, plus guns and accompanied by one of the Africans, would go out to shoot a buck. It was here that I actually drove a combine harvester, for the only time in my life!

Other friends managed farms for the owners, and one such couple were Val and Hugh Clarke. If I remember correctly, Hugh was of Welsh origin, but Val had been brought up in Kenya, her father having been a District Commissioner. Often we would visit them for Sunday lunch, sometimes playing tennis quoits on the lawn, other times all loading into one of the Jeeps and heading down to the lovely river and waterfall that was on the estate. Those who wanted to would swim, the others would just chat over a glass of wine. What wonderful memories! They float before my eyes like fireflies lighting up the night, mystical, wonderful, captured at the time and never forgotten.

African stories and characters

In Kenya at that time, everyone seemed to be a 'character'. Perhaps it was the influence of the African climate, perhaps the beauty of Kenya, but people were no longer grey, careful, cautious or sombre. I think it was here that I realised that life must be caught, captured and lived, as it is surely like the blink of an eye – it passes too soon.

We met strong characters who seemed fearless and brave. One such was my friend Joy, who with her two children lived near us at Hill School. Joy was the school matron. She had left her home city of Manchester many years before and come to Kenya with her then husband. They had two sons, one of whom was currently farming near Nakuru. Sadly, the marriage ended in divorce. Joy then met and married the love of her life and they were blissfully happy. He was a pseudo-Mau-Mau, one of those who tried to stop the violence of the Mau-Mau uprising. Normally fluent in Swahili and often other dialects, these men would try to infiltrate the Mau Mau gangs and kill them. They would blacken their bodies and assume a native African appearance. Brave men, they were usually aided by loyal Africans, who were often conversant with the oaths etc used by the Mau Mau. Owing to his role in this association, Joy's husband was often away, and like most Europeans at that time, she had strict instructions to always keep a revolver with her. Joy, however, was rather careless with her gun – she would get up in the morning and go out, leaving the gun under her pillow. Her house servant was always reprimanding her and telling her to be more careful and keep her gun with her. Often, at night, Joy would be trying to sleep, but was prevented from doing so by the noise coming from the shambas (servants' houses) at the edge of the property; she would open her window and shout to tell them 'nyamaza!' (be quiet). In 1960, after the uprising, Joy discovered why she was never harmed – her house servant had been the chief oath taker for the district and the noise was due to the number of Africans being sworn into the movement. Sadly, Joy's husband died, and she was left with two children to look after, which was why she turned back to nursing and as Matron was able to have free housing for them on the campus.

The other person I knew who was involved with the Mau Mau was the Afrikaner owner of Genevieve the mongoose; her name was Neville. She, her husband and children lived on a farm outside Eldoret. Her husband had left the country on business and she was at home with the three children when the Mau Mau broke in, brandishing pangas (enormous cutting tools rather like a machete). In order to protect her three children, Neville barred their entry to the children's bedrooms, but she was brutally attacked, and it was a miracle that help came and they saved her life. Her legs, however, bore dreadful scars.

Parents' visits

During the two years we spent there both my parents (individually) visited. When my Dad came, we took a trip to Uganda and stayed one night at Kampala before travelling on to Murchison Falls. What a wonderful holiday that was! We took a boat up to the falls and everything seemed bigger than in Kenya. The elephants were enormous, as were the crocodiles, basking on the shores with their monstrous gaping jaws exposing huge teeth which were simultaneously being cleaned by plovers which fed on the morsels of food left in the crocodiles' mouths. We saw all sorts of game and the trip right up to the falls was wonderful. Another visit was to the tea plantations at Kericho, west of the Rift Valley, at the edge of the Mau forest. Kericho's altitude and warm and temperate climate make it perfect for the production of tea.

When my mother visited, one of the sightseeing trips we made was to go down the Kerio Valley. In those days, you had to have a permit to go down, and an askari (guard) took the number of your car, so that should you have a problem and not return, they would send a search party or mechanic down to rescue you. When we were there we saw a man walking across carrying a magnificent spear in one hand and an earthenware pitcher in the other. We wanted to buy an African spear, but not one of the masses produced for tourists and displayed in Nairobi and other markets. After greeting him – I think he was a member of the Nandi tribe, although he was tall, slim, and looked very much like a Turkana, but I stupidly never asked what tribe he was from – we admired his spear and then tentatively asked if we could buy it. After much, much deliberation and a great deal of haggling, we eventually bought the lovely spear for £5. Not much now, but a great deal of money in Kenya in those days! It has always been a treasured possession.

On another occasion when we went down into the Kerio, a group of African women and children appeared. Where they came from I do not know, but suddenly they were there. The women were beautiful, with lovely smiles, elongated ear lobes and a seemingly happy nature. I think they were of the Elgeyo tribe. Their necks were adorned with rows of wires which were attached to one another and covered with kaleidoscopic beads. They were magnificent!

Sue had a doll with her and one of the group – she was obviously one of the elders –

approached and motioned that she wanted the doll. We gave it to her, and she started to dance whilst chanting a low, melodious hum. The humming gave way to raucous laughter and comments from the younger women, who joined in the laughter and strove to look at the doll. I think this must have been some sort of joke about female castration, which was then commonplace amongst the tribes, and perhaps our doll was lacking the scars. Whatever it was, the doll's female genitals were a great source of amusement.

Sadly for John, although invited, his parents never came to visit – perhaps the distance discouraged them.

Kenyan life

We did not always have to go 'on safari' to enjoy Kenya. Often, on a Sunday, a crowd of us would drive out to the Soy club for Sunday lunch. An old colonial club (I believe our present Queen stayed there whilst on honeymoon), it had a comfortable feel and the staff were always so hospitable. To reach the club we had to take the Kitale road, and I cannot remember where – I believe it was near Hoey's Bridge – there was always a troop of colobus monkeys chattering and jumping in the trees and seemingly flying with ease. Their distinctive black and white fur seemed to stand out from the foliage. I believe that these magnificent arboreal animals are now a threatened species – we were so lucky to see troops of them so often.

It was on one of these excursions when after lunch, as all the adults sat chatting over coffee whilst the children played, one of our friends' children, Mark, came running in shouting 'Dad, Dad, there's a pervert in the toilet!' Immediately his father and several other men rushed to the toilets, only to find not a pervert but a vervet monkey!

I also remember taking the children out on the Soi road to see the giraffes. A tower of them were always seen roaming here and the children used to call out 'come here, giraffes' in Swahili – 'njoo hapa twiga'. Of course, they never came, but we just loved watching those graceful animals as they strolled through the bush. Several years ago, I asked someone from Eldoret if they were still there, but I was told that the then President Arap Moi had built a big army camp there and the giraffes were moved to Nairobi Park. (Incidentally, Arap Moi was born and educated in Eldoret.) So often, in those days, the Kenya-Uganda train would have to stop near Eldoret because the giraffes were crossing or standing on the line!

So, our life continued. John would start college at 8 am and dress in trousers, top and sweater. By 10 am when he came home for his coffee break, it was time to shed the trousers and sweater and don three-quarter socks and shorts. This was the common attire for men and I always thought, and still think, that shorts and three-quarter socks look so smart on them. He had a Wednesday afternoon off and would go to Eldoret Golf Club to play in another much-loved sport. I would collect the children from their respective schools and drive to the club, where the children would swim in the pool and play with friends. After golf, John would join us and then we would order tea. For the princely sum of 2 Kenyan shillings, we were treated to a feast of delicately made sandwiches (no crusts) and a superb assortment of cakes, gateaux etc. all accompanied by pots of whichever tea you chose – all served in fine bone china, of course!

The other highlight of the week was Sunday, usually spent at Eldoret Sports Club. There were quite a few staff working there, but I always remember the head barman, whose name was Sali. He always looked immaculate in his uniform and red fez hat; his smile was infectious, and he had so much patience with all the children who were constantly ordering drinks at the bar. He used to have to stoop over to see our daughter, Sue, as she was so short, and Sali used to call her 'Memsahib kidogo' (the little memsahib). In those days, unlike now, the term 'memsahib' was in common usage.

Once a month there would be a tennis tournament, the winners getting a silver spoon. Amazingly I was given one – I am sure it was a spoon of sympathy for the person who tried the hardest! Everyone took plates of food, plus there was some provided by the club. Long trestle tables would be laden with food and there was a cacophony of noise with adults and children's chatter. Neville Rowan usually brought her mongoose and often Genevieve would manage to get onto the table and attempt to join in the meal! She was usually kept on a lead, and the girls would clamour to take Genevieve for a walk. Also, at the Sports Club there was a monthly film night, usually on a Sunday. We would all get there early and order dinner – they did an excellent steak egg and chips, I remember – all for the princely sum of approximately two shillings. The children would be dressed for bed and then put into the cars which were just outside in the car park. Lying down, on prepared bedding, they were told to go to sleep – of course, this usually meant lots of car windows being opened and lots of laughter and conversations passing between the cars. The adults could all relax and watch the film, knowing that the askari (guard) employed by the club, would ensure that no one got out of their cars and that they were all safe. Should there be any nonsense he would come in and call the parents.

I am making our life there sound totally blissful, but we had our ups and downs. Money was scarce and we were living in cramped accommodation. As an incentive to work in underdeveloped countries, the MOD put a monthly sum of money into your UK bank. Before going to Africa, we envisaged saving all this for a lump sum at the end – no such luck, as we decided that we wanted to enjoy our time in Africa, not spend it indoors and on our own. One of the many Asian shop keepers was always glad to give us Kenyan currency if we, in return, transferred sterling to one of their UK bank accounts, an arrangement which served both parties very well. John also often had weekend duty, and this meant checking on the students throughout the weekend, from start to finish of the day (it was a boarding college). He would supervise their work and their meals, and this duty often involved (during the evening/night) either cleaning up wounds (I would help) or taking them to the hospital to have stitches. This was, of course, because they would either have a few drinks, or just have disagreements!

I am afraid I have misled you by calling the students 'boys' – they were anything in age from 17-40, as education was extremely valued and difficult to obtain. I can remember John's disgust when he started teaching English there. These poor African students had been grappling with English classics such as Dickens – how appalling is that? Other books available to them were written in English FOR the English, as they were not remotely related to African life/culture. John found himself trying to explain (often accompanied by blackboard illustrations) what a double-decker bus looked like, why people used their milk in bottles, or the meaning of 'rush hour' etc. etc. I can remember him making phone calls and writing letters to the Australian and British High Commission, plus the British Council, and eventually obtaining relevant African books written in English, so that the students could understand, enjoy and simultaneously improve their English skills. Sometimes a student would have walked hundreds of miles to get to the college, only to be turned away because they did not have the required fees. The poor men would then have to walk hundreds of miles home. It was a sad situation for the Africans.

By Christmas of 1969 we had moved to a new house again. The headmaster had left (staff breathed a sigh of relief), and we were given his house. It was much larger than the small semi we were in, with a large garden and accommodation for Charles at the back, so we were in heaven. Often, when John was on duty, the boys would come up to the house to have a dressing put on a cut. I stupidly on one occasion tried to practise my Swahili on this 6ft young man. He just gave me a lovely smile and said 'Mrs Davies, I speak perfect English'. Just served me right, and I never did that again!

Excursions

Of course, we did not spend all our time in Eldoret. We made trips all over Kenya, as John oversaw the training of the college athletes – and what magnificent athletes there were! They all loved athletics and had a natural tendency in this field. I remember going to Moi, Iten, Kitale and Nakuru and naturally cheered on the Rift Valley competitors. I remember my husband being annoyed with the priests from Iten, as they were famous – or perhaps infamous – for scouring Kenya and persuading the best athletes to go to Iten, and several of the Olympic champions came from there. I believe it is now the centre for high altitude training.

Other excursions include visits to Nairobi; we all loved visiting the game park there. I can remember on one occasion being chased by an ostrich, and they can certainly run! It is not an experience I would want to repeat. We saw magnificent cheetah stalk their prey (often Impala) and then speed with graceful velocity to capture and kill; lions reclining in the late afternoon before arousing to stalk that night's dinner; graceful giraffes entwining their necks in their love dance; cheeky warthogs and snorting hippos – nature is so incredible!

We would often go, with another family, for a day out in the Aberdares, taking a picnic and sometimes fishing in a river, admiring the beauty of the gushing flow of Thompson's Falls. There were trips to Nakuru – perhaps lunch at the Stags Head and a trip to the Menegai Crater; at other times just spending the day at the lake, its vast expanse endowed with a cloak of pink – the graceful flamingos. There were also 'mad' days. I can remember one such occasion when the men decide it would be a good idea to have a race. This was not an ordinary race, but one which involved cow skins being attached to the backs of cars. On each skin a man would sit and the cars would then speed off, trying to make as many sharp turns as possible. The rear passenger would attempt to stay on the skin whilst his underside got severely burnt and bruised!

In April, there was the East African Safari, enjoyed by all, and we used to camp out to help at the check points. At altitude, the nights were cold, and I can remember shivering. The children, warmly wrapped up in the cars, usually slept most of the night whereas we stood shivering at the checkpoints whilst awaiting the next roaring car to arrive. Those nights were sleepless, but exciting!

Meeting Jomo Kenyatta

I cannot remember why the President was in Eldoret – perhaps to open a new building? I seem to remember a new Town Hall, or it may have been to open the Eldoret Show which was an annual, much celebrated event. There was a reception held in his honour and, for some reason, John and I were invited. After the reception it was almost dark, and we were ushered outside, where seating was allocated. The President and his then wife, Mama Ngina, were seated in a sort of 'box' and, to my delight, we were seated next to them, albeit just on chairs! Then the ceremony started – tribal dancing, which was both fascinating and frightening. By this time darkness had descended and although there was some sort of outside lighting, the darkness gave a sort of eeriness to the display. I can remember the warriors, adorned in huge feather headdresses which framed their faces, brandishing their enormous spears whilst simultaneously chanting and placing their feet in unison for the rhythmic, pulsating dance. As their feet struck the ground, the earth seemed to vibrate; their faces looked hypnotic, and their movements merged into one. Their eyes took on an unreal glaze, the earth resounded with their steps and it became an almost frightening experience. It was reminiscent of the untamed world of Conrad's 'Heart of Darkness'; one felt like crying out 'the horror, the horror!' yet simultaneously one was fascinated, intoxicated, hypnotised by the experience. I can remember feeling, for a moment or two, rather frightened, but fear was soon dispelled when the happy, laughing President emerged from his box and joined in the dancing.

Then there were the school/college holidays and our two visits to the coast.

Mombasa

Mombasa was unique – very Arabic, with its influences from Oman and the island of Zanzibar. In the town itself huge tusks provided an apt canopy over the main road and a myriad colourful bougainvillea cascaded over the white buildings. I remember the magnificent 16th century walls of Fort Jesus, the ocean lapping at its perimeters and the graceful dhows, bringing their wares and often carrying beautiful Zanzibar wooden chests. It had its own unique character which segregated it from the rest of Kenya.

Our first visit to the coast was during our first Christmas in Kenya – 1968. We decided to go with our friends Malcolm and Grace Nicholls and their daughter Becky. John and Malcolm hired a very large tent – big enough to accommodate four adults and three children. We also hired sleeping bags and with high spirits off we set. The length of the journey from Eldoret to the coast (almost 500 miles), travelling on murram roads, plus having three young children, necessitated two overnight stops.

Our first was at Lake Naivasha. Setting up the tent was a mammoth task, as neither Malcolm nor I had a clue about camping, whereas our partners were experienced campers. Consequently, we just did as we were told and helped. I remember us going somewhere to eat, but the experience of camping there was not good – the lake attracted too many mosquitoes.

The next day we set off for our next stop, Tsavo Game Park. We loved it here. We did a game drive in the afternoon and then sat on the veranda of the lodge having a cool drink and watching the game flock to the waterhole in front of us. Wonderful, we thought. Then came the task of erecting the tent once more. We were directed to the camping area and shown where there was wood we could use for our fire. Tent in situ, the men made a huge bonfire on which we could put our saucepans of soup and beans.

How naive were we! No sooner had we started to cook than we were enveloped by a huge swarm of flying ants – they must have been attracted by the heat and light. Our saucepans were soon covered in black ants. We made a hasty retreat into our tent and closed the zips – we were going to bed hungry that night. Not only were we hungry, but we were kept awake as a cackle of hyenas decided to surround us, and their howls were piercing!

The next morning, we headed to the north coast of Mombasa. The parent of one of Malcolm's Hill School pupils owned an hotel here called Ocean Sports. It was a centre for fishing enthusiasts and was fronted by the beautiful white sand of Watamu bay. The kind hotelier was allowing us to camp on the beach and had said we could use the hotel's facilities. We were delighted! White sands, swaying palms, use of toilets and showers, plus an excellent restaurant – what more could we want? I still remember the succulent lobster I had that night for dinner and John proclaimed it the best barracuda he had ever tasted! All was perfect – well, almost perfect. Have you ever tried sleeping on sand? I would not recommend it. Stupidly, we had gone camping without camp beds, and the sand was even more uncomfortable than the hard ground!

The next day we explored North Coast a little and then decided to head for the South Coast, where we intended to spend most of our holiday. Of course, Mombasa is an island and to get to the camping site we had chosen you had to get the Likoni ferry. In those days, the ferry was not as large or as crowded as today, but it was large enough to accommodate vehicles. Driving on to it was a real adventure for the children, but we had left it late, just catching the last ferry, and by the time we landed it was almost dark.

Following our directions, we arrived at the site at Tiwi beach – a huge field. There were quite a few tents already in situ, and we thought they looked a little crowded together, but at the front edge of the field there was no one. We decided to pitch there and, with the aid of car lights the tent was erected. We went for a walk on the sandy beach in front of us and with the aid of torches admired what seemed like hundreds of hermit crabs scuttling across the sand. After eating, tired but happy, we all settled down for the night.

The following morning, awakening incredibly early, we all realised why the other campers had avoided our position. They had lots of shade from the many palm trees – we had none, and that tent was SO hot! Consequently, we left Tiwi and headed south, to Diani. Finding a more suitable site, we pitched the tent and settled in. We spent the days just swimming or trying to find somewhere cool – we loved Diani beach and were able to use the only hotel and beach bar to keep cool, have decent food and long, ice-cold drinks. This was my first experience of snorkelling – I am not a good swimmer. Encouraged by my husband, I put on the snorkel and went out to where there were deep pools just inside the coral reef. The sight was amazing! Not only coral, but wonderful kaleidoscopic fish. Watching them swim, darting in and out of the equally colourful coral, was a wonderful, never-to-be-forgotten sight.

Our next visit was the following summer, but on this occasion, we went with three other families. A surgeon in Nairobi had a daughter living in Eldoret, and through her we were able to rent his very large Mombasa house. I can remember it was virtually divided in two, with a narrow dirt open corridor running between the front and rear halves of the house. The rear housed the servants' quarters, the kitchen and bathroom. The front had a combined hall/lounge and the bedrooms. We had paid the train fare for two of our house servants to come with us – I think that Charles was delighted to come, and the only chores were for them to cook the meals.

I can still envisage what that first night there was like. Again, we had caught the ferry and by the time we landed it was again dark. The road on South Island at that time was very narrow, a simple dirt road approximately the width of a car. It was nick-named the 'chicken run', as you had to try to avoid any oncoming traffic. Following directions, we arrived at the left turning for the house; I distinctly remember the dirt road seeming to disappear – we must have been elevated above the house. On descending, and with the aid of the car lights, we saw the house on our left. Making our way onto the large veranda our eyes rested on a pair of very old magnificent Arab doors. Rapping on these, we heard approaching footsteps from inside – you must remember it was pitch dark. Slowly, with a creaking groan (reminiscent of a ghost film), the door opened, held by a turbaned Arab gentleman who was holding aloft a large lantern. This was, we discovered, the rather frightening resident 'warden' or housekeeper.

After finding our bedrooms – we had a large one which we shared with our children – we settled down for a night's sleep, only to be awakened by a terrific noise on the corrugated tin roof, firstly from the monkeys and then, during the night, by a torrential downpour. The latter necessitated us getting out of our beds and moving them, as the roof leaked!

At least on this visit we had beds, and after a good night's sleep we awoke to paradise. Everything looked so much better in daylight. The house had an enormous front balcony on which were chairs and tables. Just outside was a small grove of palm trees and we could hear the waves lapping on the shore.

Charles and the other house servant had arrived before us and that morning we were treated to a fine breakfast of pawpaw, pineapple, eggs, and toast. Outside the house was a path leading down to our own private cove, inhabited by no one else except the resident monkeys – it was idyllic! Charles enjoyed it all and would swim everyday. I always wondered where he learnt to swim – it must have been in some of the up-country rivers. We only ventured out for a change of beach, usually to Diani, which had, at that time, just one thatched hotel, but most days we enjoyed our cove and the company of friends. Each morning a local fisherman would call with a basket containing the daily catch and we were able to feast on beautiful fresh fish and crustaceans.

This was not an extravagant holiday in a luxurious hotel, but it was one of the most memorable and enjoyable holidays I have ever had. It is not luxury that matters – just location!

Life went on as normal, tennis spoons, excursions etc. I loved all aspects of our life there: the crisp early morning dew; the rapidity of the sun descending in the evenings; the warmth of a log fire at night; the Ibis as they landed on our lawn and pierced the ground with their long, pointed beaks; the sounds of the drums from a nearby village when the inhabitants drank pombe and had a 'chama' (party); the perfume of the mimosa which grew just outside our balcony – I just did not want to leave! I begged John to stay on for another contract. He was offered the role of head, but his position in Port Talbot had been kept open for him and he was convinced that had we stayed, it would only be for a short time before the post was occupied by an African.

CHAPTER 4

Farewell to Africa

Trying to find homes for our dear pets was a particularly traumatic time for me. The whole episode still brings pain to me when I recall what happened.

A new member of staff at the college had offered to have our lovely cat, Fluffy. He and his wife lived in a flat at the Hill School. We took her to the flat, together with her basket etc. Unbeknown to me, Fluffy soon disappeared, and I only found out a few weeks later. On making enquiries, I was told that a stray cat had been seen behind Loreto Convent. I went to that area and spent hours wandering in the vast open space, all the time calling to the cat. Eventually I heard this very weak cry and there, looking starved and ill, was our lovely cat. I picked her up, took her home and attempted to give her some milk, but she was so weak. We called the vet and on seeing Fluffy, he said she had suffered from cat flu and needed to be put to sleep. I was SO upset. If only the couple had told us she had gone missing (we later found out she escaped on the first day), she might not have died.

Next was our lovely dog Tramp. I asked so many Europeans if they would take her, but no one seemed to want a dog. I had an offer from one of the African workers on the compound, but Africans treat animals as animals, rather than pets, and Tramp was used to being a much-loved pet. Finally, we had to make the decision to have her put to sleep. John offered to take her, but I declined. I said, 'she is my dog, so I will stay with her'. I later took Tramp into Eldoret and I can remember stupidly walking around and approaching Europeans to see if they would take her. Having no success I took her into the vet and held her paw, tears streaming, while she was put to sleep.

Then there was my lovely Kali. A parrot is easily transportable by plane and I begged John to let me take her back to the UK. Unlike me, John was not an animal lover; he would not harm an animal, but was happy to live without any pets. He was adamant and said no way were we taking the parrot back. It so happened that my friend Joy Trafford was about to leave Kenya for a new position in what was then Southern Rhodesia (now Zimbabwe). She had accepted the role of Matron at the Victoria Falls hospital. A strong character, Joy was driving her little VW Beetle from Eldoret to Zimbabwe (almost 3000 kms) with her two children and their luggage. A daring feat for a woman alone in Africa. Joy said that they would happily take Kali. I was delighted, as I knew she would be looked after, and she would stay in Africa. I can clearly remember waving them off as they left, with Kali in her cage on the back seat. Sadly, many months later I discovered that Kali had grieved, lost all her feathers and died. I never forgave John for not allowing me to bring her with us.

So, at the end of the summer 1970, we said goodbye to friends and Charles and, with suitcases overfull, we got into our 'matatu' to make the journey to Nairobi airport. I cried most of the way. I think I knew it would be years before I returned to Kenya.

Our return to Britain, 1970

Although it was a bright July day when we arrived in Port Talbot, everything looked grey; the roofs, the houses, even the people did not look colourful! I can distinctly remember Nigel saying, 'I know, why don't all the Africans come here to live and all the British go to Africa?' Out of the mouths of children... I think we felt the same.

We moved back into our house and with the little gratuity left we installed central heating and bought a new sofa. We decided that we would put both children into private school as a precaution should we decide, a year later, to return abroad. Both attended Porthcawl schools, Sue to the Convent and Nigel to St. John's boys' school. Once they had settled in, I knew I needed to work to pay school fees, plus I was bored. Seeing a position that appealed to me advertised in the local press, I decided to apply. It was for a personnel officer at a local factory which employed about 400 people. I thought I would hear no more, but to my great surprise I was offered an interview, and I was even more surprised when I was given the position. I found that job varied and interesting and loved the human interaction. I worked there for two or three years, but then my father had some health problems, and my mother was finding running the business on her own very difficult. Sadly, I gave in my notice and went to assist in the business.

I finally decided it was time to get some 'A' levels and further my education, so I attended the college two evenings a week and took 'A' level English and Sociology. I really enjoyed both subjects and passed them the following June.

By this time, we could not envisage going abroad again – John had applied and been accepted for a position with an oil company, at a fantastic salary. The company was prepared to give all sorts of incentives, including paying for the children's school fees. My father and I took Nigel to Brecon School, where he sat and passed the entrance exam. He also had an interview with the headmaster, who later told John in a telephone conversation that Nigel was very unhappy about us going abroad and leaving him in the UK. I had already sold some furniture (thinking that we were leaving), but that night we literally 'paced the boards' and decided that we could not go. A much-relieved son and a disappointed mother, but that was the decision we made. We did, however, decide that it was time for us to 'upgrade' in the housing market and buy a detached property.

With the unlikelihood of us leaving the UK, we had transferred the children to the local schools, and both were students at Glanafan Comprehensive. I had seen a house for sale near to the town and within walking distance of their school. We viewed, liked, and bought. The house had a pair of semi-detached properties next to it and was approached via a long drive which went past the grounds and tennis court, all of which belonged to us. It sounds very grand, but the tennis court needed some work and we used it mainly as a car park.

I also decided to make use of my 'A' levels and applied to Swansea University. I was accepted as an undergraduate on a single Honours English degree course. I absolutely loved my time there and even though I was much older than most of the students, I got on very well with them. Towards the end of the first year, having completed all my assignments and gained particularly good grades, I stupidly became over overridden with guilt. The children were now both teenagers and I felt that they were being deprived of things because I was not contributing to the household – perhaps the new house and larger mortgage also had an influence. I decided to leave university. It was a stupid decision and one I have always regretted. Had I just sat my exams I could then have completed, at a future date, a degree in two rather than three years. I shall never forget that some of my fellow students, much younger than I, took the trouble to come from Swansea to try to persuade me to change my mind. Nevertheless, I looked for work and found an interesting position in the Civil Service as assistant to the Occupational Psychologist and Social Worker at the local Rehabilitation Centre.

This house move became the first of many; I often wonder if we had some nomadic blood in us. Each relocation involved home improvements, from new kitchen/bathroom to new roofs and windows, and we usually made the upheaval, work and mess economically beneficial. Conversely, we also lost money on property – our house in Carmarthenshire, our property in France and latterly my home in Wales.

I am jumping ahead. It was while we were living in this house that we took our first holiday abroad. I found a gîte in the Cognac region of France, in a tiny hamlet on the outskirts of the village of Cozes. We were all extremely excited and once we embarked on the ferry we were 'abroad'. I cannot remember much of our journey through France, apart from it being very pleasant (we took the minor roads) and I think we had an overnight stop. On arrival at our gîte we were warmly welcomed by Madame Gosselin. The gîte was in the grounds of their large property, which housed the entire extended family and accommodated their offices, distillery, and the 'caves' for the 'dégustations'.

On the first night we were invited to the house of the younger Gosselins – Monsieur, Madame, their eldest child Dominique and their daughter Sylvie, with whom Sue struck up a friendship. Our 'bienvenu' seemed, initially, quite formal; we all sat around the large circular table whilst Madame ceremoniously cut and distributed the cake she had made. Whilst we were eating Monsieur kept making furtive glances toward the huge dresser, whilst Madame simultaneously gave him disapproving looks. We eventually found the reason for their behaviour: Monsieur could not wait to demonstrate to us, with great pride, the fruit of his labours, the much-prized Cognac, whilst Madame obviously did not approve of too much alcohol! We were each given a glass of the superb Cognac, the ladies having a smaller amount, whilst Sylvie and Sue were each given a sugar cube in a spoon, over which was poured the golden liquid.

A delightful welcome and a wonderful first trip abroad as a family, but sadly the only one, as in subsequent years Nigel chose to holiday with friends. On this trip, however, he spotted a nightclub in the tiny hamlet (a strange location for a nightclub, we thought) and begged to be allowed to go. We consented, and showered and smartly dressed, off he set. Although we had consented, we could not rest until he was home. Rural France is very black at night and Nigel did not take a torch, but despite this he found his way back to the gîte. We heard a rapturous account of his evening and the décor of the club, which, we were told, had a swimming pool behind the bar!

Sue and Sylvie went for bike rides in the French countryside; grandmère Gosselin would call on her way back from the vegetable garden and supply us with salad and delicious French beans. There were trips to the Gironde, Cognac, and Royan. Of course, we could not stay with a family who produced superb Cognac without having the tour, the usual 'dégustation', consuming some whilst there and buying quite a few bottles to bring home!

We kept in touch and visited again the following year. I remember that by the next summer Dominique had married, and a new baby had arrived. I took out a white baby suit as a present and later Madame sent me a photo of Dominique's son at his christening, dressed in the gift we had given.

I mentioned that the house we had bought had a large garden as well as a tennis court. The areas John hated the most were those alongside the curved drive. Apart from trees, ground cover plants had been long established and try as he might, John had a continual battle in trying to control them. On our return from France John was aghast – the whole area seemed to have gone wild again, and he immediately came to the decision that he wanted to sell. We settled in and then phoned a local estate agent who visited the next day, said he knew of someone who would like the property and lo and behold, the following day we had sold! Most sensible people would look for a house before putting their current abode on the market – not us. We now started the search for a new home.

John saw a cottage for sale on Pen-y-Cae Road, the area in which he spent his childhood. Perhaps he had the same feelings about that as I had about Baglan, because I know that as soon as we viewed, he wanted to buy. It was a lovely, detached cottage, but had lots of disadvantages, which I vehemently pointed out: it had only two bedrooms, needed new windows and a new kitchen, and had no garage or car parking.

My arguments fell on stony ground. John was determined we would buy. Poor Nigel had to suffer whilst we literally built his bedroom around him; there followed a new kitchen, lovely new traditional style double glazed windows etc. The house had lots of character and was conveniently situated for John and me, Sue's school, and Nigel's work in the bank. By this time Nigel and passed his test and had a flashy car; I seem to remember it was a bright yellow colour. He was also supplementing his bank salary by working in a garage at weekends and his love of cars made him an enthusiastic and persuasive car salesman!

We stayed in the cottage for several years, but I was never happy there and it is the only house I have ever lived in where I felt there was a 'presence '. It may seem unreal and stupid, but Sue also had the same feeling. It was also a time when there were a few marital problems (all marriages have them). Perhaps that added to my feeling of wanting to relocate. There are, however, happy memories. Sue passed her 'A' levels with flying colours and Nigel had met Judith, who was to become his wife and mother of our three grandchildren, so there were good memories as well as bad.

I then heard that a house I had known since my childhood was for sale, in the location of my childhood, Baglan. The owner of the house, Cynthia, had been married to Hugh, one of my mother's brothers, to whom I was particularly close. I obviously knew his ex-wife very well, so I phoned and told her we might be interested in the property. She then came to see me, we chatted, and a viewing was arranged.

The rest is history. We viewed, liked and bought. We were

incredibly happy there; on looking back I wonder why we ever sold, but one cannot look back, decisions are made when they are made, and once made, they are the right decisions. Had we not sold this property our lives might have been quite different.

My first memories of Ty'r Eglwys are of when I visited there as a child. I remember the family and the house as it was then. It was still a farm then, although not a very active one. It still owned a great deal of the land in Baglan and because of this Cynthia's grandfather had the nickname 'Tom Baglan'. The house was then in its original state. A few steps off the kitchen, but part of it, was a door leading into the pantry. It had a slate floor and a thick slate shelf across the width of the area. On here milk and meat would be kept and jellies put to set. My memories of Cynthia's parents are vivid. Her mother Vi (short for Violet) ran the house; a tall, well-built woman, she was more than capable of farm life. I can remember her making the pig swill in the kitchen and I would go with her, through the large, long gardens, through the kissing gate to the pigsties. I hated the bantam chickens that were always running around – I was always a little afraid of them. Cynthia's father was a slim, quiet man – I think the rest of the family overpowered him, though he always had a kindly smile for me. I remember him sitting alone at the kitchen table eating bread and cheese. Her grandfather, the famous, or should it be infamous, Tom Baglan, who was obviously the head of the household, seemed to be sitting in perpetuity beside the fire in the dining room smoking his pipe. His wife, to my memory, was always in bed – perhaps she was bedridden? She used to wear a very old-fashioned nightcap on her head, and I can remember the stone hot water bottle being taken into her bedroom. I heard, many years later, that Tom had not become celibate because of his bedridden wife, as he had had a long-term affair with one of the female Baglan residents. There was another member of the family, who I think was Vi's brother. I believe he had some mental problems and he lived apart from the family, but in a bungalow on another of their fields and not far away from the farm. The property had a front veranda and was named 'The Brambles'. It was demolished many years later to make way for new houses.

Alongside the main farmhouse was another kissing gate which led to a huge field. The family must have maintained echoes of farming, as I can remember going into that field and helping with the hay collection. Baglan was, at that time, sparsely populated and being elevated, the field had the most fantastic views over Baglan Bay. Many years later, after Cynthia had inherited the house and all the land attached to it, that field, along with others, was sold either to property developers or as individual building plots.

The house was aptly named Ty'r Eglwys because of its proximity to Baglan Church. Indeed, the area which housed the pigsties and was later to become the vegetable garden was directly above and beside the old 12th century church of St. Baglan, sadly destroyed by fire in 1954. I can remember the old church very well and often, after Sunday School, my friend Brenda and I would open the old, weathered, creaky door and enter the church. We loved to pretend we were the Llewellyns of Baglan Hall – the aristocracy of Baglan, and we would sit in the front boxed pews and try to behave graciously. I can remember Miss Llewellyn arriving at St. Catherine's Church, Baglan, and when I was young, she would arrive in a chauffeur-driven car; the other memory I have of the Llewellyns is of walking every summer to their beautiful 16th century residence for the annual Baglan fete. The grounds of the hall were beautiful, and I can remember huge rhododendron bushes. Within the shrubberies there would always be a sort of model railway, on which children could purchase a ride. We would always walk to the hall, either by taking a short cut through the woods or by going via the main road and passing by the gamekeeper's lodge – I think his name was Mr. Styles.

Again, I digress from my story; we went to Ty'r Eglwys for a viewing. We still knew it well, as when Hugh was living there, we were regular visitors. He had really worked hard on the house and garden and it was updated and transformed, with no expense spared. Sadly, it was now looking rather tired. The expensive kitchen had been neglected and look rather worn and dark; the aluminium windows were cold and draughty; the teak conservatory was shabby, and the wood had decayed. The grounds, including the two fishponds, needed attention. It was still a beautiful house with extensive grounds and a garage that looked more like a bungalow, perched at the top of a long drive,

Cynthia wanted to sell quickly – her then boyfriend wanted them to move to Marbella and she had already purchased a property there. We bought the house at a good price, sold the cottage, and moved in.

Again, we worked on the property. New windows, new roof, new kitchen plus the usual decorating and finally a new conservatory. The ponds were cleaned and stocked, the gardens maintained, and the house was a lovely home.

Of course, by now our two children had grown up. Nigel and Judith were an item, Sue had completed her 'A' levels and was accepted at University to train as a teacher. Nigel was now the business manager for a large car company, and I had finally decided to get my degree, and was studying at Swansea for a BA. It was from Ty'r Eglwys that Nigel got married – at Saint Catherine's Church, where John and I and my parents before us had married. It was a wonderful day, Sue was one of the bridesmaids and our next-door neighbours from our first Baglan house attended the wedding. I can remember Tudor, the husband, making a lovely speech – good friendships mean a lot. Prior to the big day I had spent hours and hours cooking in the kitchen; lots of the desserts bore fruits grown in our vegetable garden. When we bought the property, it included the enormous Jacobean dining table – we left it there for the subsequent owners – but it was truly of gigantic proportions and needed a huge dining room to house it. On the night of the wedding, friends and family were invited to a pre-honeymoon party. My weeks of cooking/freezing were rewarded. The huge table was laden with savouries and sweets which were quickly replenished as needed. John operated the bar and a wonderful evening culminated with the honeymoon couple driving down the hill from our house amidst a cacophony of noise, cheers and good wishes and the rattling of cans attached to the car – it was a happy conclusion to a lovely day. Clearing up the following morning necessitated walking around the garden collecting wine glasses which had been discarded by some of the guests!

Some other important events whilst living in T'yr Eglwys: I gained a 2:1 degree at the age of 43; Sue gained a 2:1 one at Southampton; and I had started working as a Field Officer with West Glamorgan Education Authority, which was interesting and involved driving around West Glamorgan monitoring or interviewing both students and employers and making reports, dealing with any problems etc. John was a Director at the College and there was a new principal who had, initially, come on his own, while his wife settled their affairs in their previous location. As he was alone, we had invited him, on several occasions, for dinner. On one such night he kept asking me about training schemes, adult education etc. etc. I was then advised to apply for a new position – to be the Tutor on the newly created Adult Rehabilitation Scheme. I found the post both challenging and immensely rewarding, as it boosted confidence and found employment for so many who had 'given up'. I was placed at a centre apart from the College but was employed by them and responsible to them.

A year or two later a vacancy occurred in the college for an 'A' level Sociology lecturer. I applied, was interviewed, and accepted the position. Another person took on my role as tutor in the JTS (Job Training Scheme), but my experience here stood me in good stead when, in addition to my lecturing role I became the co-ordinator and personal tutor for the newly formed Access to Higher Education course which focused on helping adults who had, for various reasons, previously been unable to achieve their full potential in the academic world. I was also on the Welsh committee for this scheme, and I found the work both stimulating and extremely rewarding – it was wonderful to see people being able to achieve their dreams and gain personal satisfaction whilst doing so.

Sue had been teaching in London, and said she wanted to have three years' experience in the city before applying for positions abroad. John and I made plenty of trips to the capital, sometimes armed with brushes and paint, as she was living with a college friend in a basement flat which needed 'brightening'. We found a wonderful French restaurant nearby which proved extremely useful on those weekends! Sue then applied for a teaching post with the oil company Shell, was successful and was preparing for a new chapter in her life, one that would be the start of a great deal of happiness and travelling the world.

I can remember the day that she received the phone call from Shell and we were both excited at what was ahead for her – new experiences, travel and the opportunity to widen her teaching experience. Shell was paying for her to stay in London the night before the flight, along with a few other new employees. She had been told that she would have two return business class flights to the UK each year, but John and I persuaded her not to use both to come back and visit us, but to exchange one for travel elsewhere – this was her opportunity to explore the world. This she did, and I am so glad. She was able to celebrate one of her birthdays sitting on the white sands of the Maldives; she visited her cousin in Perth, trekked through the Himalayas, toured India, travelled through Canada, and still came home once a year. On the day we took her to London I was emotional, and I think this was because I realised that I had finally lost my 'baby'. Yes, she had taught in London for three years, but there had been regular visits both by us to her and vice versa – this was a different stage in her life.

Two quite sad events happened whilst we lived here. In June 1988 John's mother asked us to take his parents to Newport, where his father was to have a hearing test regarding an extra pension. We took them and the waiting room was full. We decided to go for a short walk and left them there. Within a short time whilst we were strolling outside, John's mother screamed to us to come – his father had collapsed and sadly, died. It was a horrible day, not only because his father died, but having to follow the ambulance to the hospital, identify him and sadly take his mother home, alone. The other sad event was that my father had started to develop Alzheimer's disease, and it was heart-breaking to see it progress.

On a much brighter note, later in June 1988 our first grandson, Nicholas, was born and we were immensely proud and delighted grandparents.

We bought a nice caravan and enjoyed exploring different regions of France. Sue accompanied us on some of these trips and we loved those holidays – the delightful French countryside, the history, the food and of course, the wine! We visited Amboise, in the Loire and the residence of Leonardo da Vinci; the medieval towns of Rocamadour and Bergerac; further west the Burgundian city of Dijon with its limestone timbered houses; the cobbled courtyards and 18th century facades of lovely Besançon; delightful Normandy with its culinary delights, including moules, oysters, wonderful cheeses and cider – oh, such delightful memories! I remember telling John that one day, I would love to buy a house in France, not realising that one day, we would.

It was while we were living in Ty'r Eglwys that we took our first trip to Cyprus. I can remember it was a bitterly cold January – I seem to remember snow, and John and I were relaxing on a Sunday afternoon in the lounge, seated beside a roaring fire. Reading the Sunday paper, I browsed through the holiday lets and saw a cottage available in a village just outside Kyrenia, in Northern Cyprus. It aroused my appetite, and after showing it and discussing with John, I rang the owner. By the next day we had reserved the cottage for two weeks the following summer. We were really looking forward to seeing somewhere new, to embracing new cultures and having some Mediterranean cuisine and experiencing the Turkish Cypriot culture.

Life continued, with the usual chores, pleasures, worries (my father's Alzheimer's was getting worse), but our young grandson, Nicholas, was growing up and he gave us so much joy. It was from Ty'r Eglwys that Nicholas had been christened, and I was a proud grandma holding him that day. He absolutely worshipped John and if John was outside painting, Nick would be with him. If Bampa (Nick's name for him) was hosing the garden, Nick would have to hold the hose; we would watch the fish in the ponds, and he would hide behind one of the trees while I pretended to have difficulty in finding him. One of his favourite TV programmes was 'Ninja Turtle', so on John's birthday I bought a 'Ninja Turtle' iced cake, and we had a party in the garden.

By now my father was in care three days a week and I remember we arranged for him to stay in for one of the weeks that we were away in Cyprus. Sue, at this time, was in Oman, and due to come home in the summer. Delighted to know we were going to North Cyprus, she decided to come over and stay with us before we all returned to the UK. Unbeknown to us, this was to be the start of our love for Northern Cyprus and our life there.

With my grandparents on holiday in Paignton, 1950

With grandparents

With rex

Bridesmaids at Aunt May's wedding

With my parents at Ty'r Eglwys

Great Aunt Bopa

With my uncles Malcolm and Roy

First year in Grammar School

Our wedding, December 26th 1960

Wedding day with parents

About to leave for Kenya

Welcome to Eldoret

Our house in Kenya

With Nigel and Sue in Kenya

With children and Tramp

Our house servant Charles

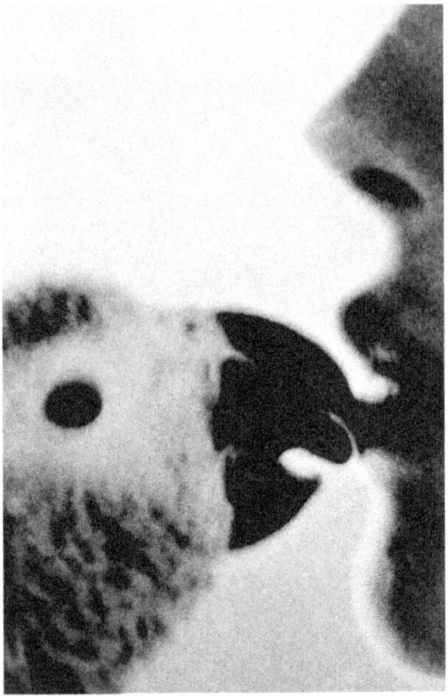

Kali giving me a kiss

Students at Rift Valley Technical College

My Dad with Kali

Young Nigel

Sue ready for school

Mombasa beach

John with children at Diani beach

Children at Mombasa

Graduating at 43 yrs of age

CHAPTER 5

Home and abroad

Northern Cyprus

In the summer of 1991, we flew from London and after a stop in Istanbul, eventually arrived in Ercan airport, which at that time was very small. We had pre-arranged a taxi to take us to the house we were renting. It was already dark, and we were quite apprehensive. It seemed a long way from the main road and we were continually driving around bends whilst simultaneously climbing up and up the mountain.

On arriving at the house, we made a quick inspection, drank a glass of wine and settled in for the night. Sue was arriving the next afternoon and we had a hire car being delivered the following morning. All paperwork done for the car, we decided we would familiarise ourselves with the village and after some shopping we would collect Sue from Ercan.

We were taken aback by the beauty of the village of Karmi, sometimes called Karaman. It had narrow, sometimes sloping roads, some with steps. There were cobbled alleyways and whitewashed, usually flat-roofed houses, flowers peeping out of the steps seemingly fighting to reach the sun; walls covered with the vibrant colours of bougainvillea – golden, pink, vibrant red and the more common purple. They bloomed everywhere and contrasted with the gleaming white of the walls.

We found the small village shop and introduced ourselves to the friendly owner, Tony; located the nearby bar (Spot) and the pub, aptly named 'The Crow's Nest' as it looked down on the beautiful coastline. Just up the narrow road from the shop was an old-fashioned red telephone box and alongside this were some old foot-worn steps, leading up to the square and the magnificent Greek Church. It was SO beautiful, and the cascading bougainvillea reminded me of Mombasa. I remember turning to John and saying, 'this is the nearest we shall ever get to going back to Africa'.

That afternoon we drove back to the airport, and on the way we were able both to find our bearings and admire the magnificent scenery. Karaman was 300m above sea level and nestled beneath the beautiful Besparmak (five fingers) mountains. The village, formerly an EOKA stronghold, had been abandoned during the uprising of 1974 and in 1982 the Turkish Cypriot authorities, on the suggestion of a European lady named Nadia Brunton, decided to offer the properties on a lease basis to people who would renovate, under certain controls, the ruined houses. The houses were let on a 49-year lease, and renovation rules were strict and ensured that the unique character of the village was retained.

The lovely, but sometimes formidable Nadia, whom we later got to know very well, took on the responsibility of overseeing the renovation of the wonderful Greek church, and it was done with care and respect. Later, Nadia would tirelessly light the candles on a Sunday and sit in the church with its doors open for anyone who wanted to view it or pray within its peaceful enclaves. For those who were interested, she would also relate the history of the village. Her whole life was focused on ensuring that the history of Karmi and its preservation for the future would be guaranteed.

As we drove down the hill, learning to cope with the numerous bends, we could admire not only the scenery but the nearest buildings. We passed a small but beautiful Greek church, opposite which was seemingly a 'smallholding'. There was a wonderful old lady dressed in black, her body bent over the stick she held, and she stood there alongside her flock but finding time to turn her head, smile and wave to us as we passed. We then came to the tiny hamlet of Edremit, drove past the village shop and waved to the large, smiling owner who sat outside his basket shop – such an array of different shapes and colours. From small to large, for shopping, for flowers, for laundry, he had basketware for every occasion!

Down again we went until we came to the small town or village of Karaoglanoglu. Here we turned right and headed along past the turning to Girne (Kyrenia) and again, a spectacular drive through the mountains, descending onto the Mesaoria Plain, a vast, quite arid expanse of land in contrast to the lush vegetation of the mountains.

In those days Ercan airport was small, and you were able to

go upstairs and out onto the balcony to see the planes land. I was so excited to see Sue get off the plane that day and it was the beginning of a wonderful and eventful holiday.

That night we ate at the Crow's Nest and the next day we took Sue on a tour of the village. We had already been told some of the history of Karmi and how people had obtained their properties. On walking down the hill past the pub we saw a seemingly restored house for sale. We contacted Ian Smith, the estate agent, and viewed. It was cheap, but I would hardly have called it renovated! It was basically one room upstairs, which was the sitting area, and an opening in the floor accommodated a wooden ladder which led to the one downstairs bedroom; this, in turn, had an outside door leading to a 'long-drop' toilet. There was a small, overgrown area which could, in the loosest terms, be called a 'garden', but we were attracted by the price – at least, it was, at a stretch, something we could afford. John's imagination was working overtime and from that moment, he began to spend time measuring the existing building and drawing plans for renovation. Sue was also enthusiastic, and after much discussion, we put in an offer, which was accepted.

The rest of the holiday was a whirl. We explored the coastline, walked through the scenic mountains to the next village (Ilgaz), discovered the 'haute cuisine' of the Levant restaurant in Karmi, and loved spending time in the picturesque harbour of Kyrenia. Surrounded by old carob warehouses (now restaurants, apartments, and hotels), the harbour is guarded by the magnificent castle, the origins of which go back to the Romans in the first century AD, but it was mainly built and modified by the Venetians in the 14th century. I never tired of sitting here in the evening, having a pre-prandial drink whilst listening to the

Muezzin as his voice calls from the turret of the mosque, its sound echoing over the whole of Kyrenia.

The two weeks we were there went by in a flash. John worked on designing what alterations we wanted done to the house. His designs culminated in a lounge separated from the kitchen/diner by an archway and a few steps. Off the lounge was a large roof terrace, flanked by waist-high walls and affording fantastic views of the mountains, the coast and St. Hilarion Castle. The lounge, though not large, had a small fireplace in one corner, and the huge arched window/doors leading on to the terrace were a feature of the room. From the lounge led a spiral staircase going down to a small hall, with a shower room/toilet on one side and a double bedroom on the other. Ahead was the master bedroom, which had French windows leading out to the garden, where we planned to have a raised flower bed, patio, and steps leading up to the small front courtyard.

We were introduced to Hassan Al Bayrak, a Turkish builder who lived in the village. We saw his work and approved it, so we left a series of post-dated cheques with our estate agent, Ian Smith, and, with Sue, and headed back to the UK. We also left strict instructions with Hassan that the house was to be finished by Easter of the following year, when we would be coming for two weeks. It was a remarkably busy but wonderful holiday with a totally unplanned result! How impetuous we were, but we made the right decision.

After a lovely summer with Sue, and telling our rather shocked parents what we had done, life returned to normal. Sue went back to Oman and we promised to visit at Christmas. In the meantime, Nigel had moved firstly to Bridgend, and then to Cheltenham.

Our purchase in Cyprus led to us rethinking our lives. John pointed out that if we were now going to spend most spring and summer holidays in Cyprus, Ty'r Eglwys was not the house to own. There was too much ground to maintain, which would make leaving it for prolonged periods virtually impossible. We had to make a choice – holidays in the sun or keep our lovely house. We chose the former, and sold, but I did it with some misgivings as it was a lovely property with lots of happy memories. I still remember the sadness I felt the last time I closed the gates to the drive.

As we were moving, we decided to look further west, where we were in a quieter and more rural area. We decided to buy a new property with no work needed and bought a place in a village just outside Carmarthen. We had easy access to the motorway, so travelling to the college did not prove a problem.

First visit to Oman

I think this must have been December 1991, as I remember it being the time of the Gulf War. We were SO excited – not only to be seeing our daughter, but seeing where she lived and the country where she was living. Colleagues in the college thought we were crazy – 'What, flying to Oman in the middle of the war? You could be shot down, are you mad?' Not at all deterred, we took our flight and arrived safely in Muscat, where our daughter was waiting to greet us.

We drove through Muscat and were very impressed at the wide, clean roads. There seemed to be men at every corner, using ordinary sweeping brushes to clear any speck of dirt. The highways were flanked with varicoloured flowers, shrubs and trees and there were roundabouts with magnificent displays, fountains and so on. Sue took us to the Shell compound, which was more like a small town, with its private beach, golf course, shops, restaurants etc. her apartment was spacious, with two bedrooms. a nicely furnished lounge/dining room and, if the weather permitted (ie cool enough), an outside veranda on which to sit. She introduced us to her boyfriend, David (pronounced the Dutch way, Dahvid), as he was from Holland. A tall, blond extremely nice chap who had gained his Masters in the UK and had a good position with Shell. They had obviously become an 'item' and as David had a large three-bedroomed bungalow on the campus, we often had the apartment to ourselves.

We had such a wonderful holiday! During this, and a subsequent trip, Sue made sure that we visited some amazing places. Oman is a mixture of the new – very modern hotels, restaurants, shopping malls, alongside places of historical interest, amazing features of nature, and people still practising the crafts and skills of generations.

On this first holiday we had a traditional Christmas lunch at David's (Sue and I helped) and David had invited another Shell employee who was on his own. Prior to the lunch we all met with some other friends and opened champagne on the lovely beach. We had an amazing day which culminated in Sue announcing that she had a special anniversary gift for us (our wedding anniversary was Boxing Day). We were told to pack enough for a three-day two-night break and include swimwear plus 'nice' evening attire. She eventually gave us the reservation – it was for a break in the Al Bustan Palace Hotel, which at that time had been named as the best hotel in the world by *Leader*s magazine.

The next morning, she and David drove us to the hotel. It was approached via the usual wide, immaculate roads, and just before the entrance to the hotel the roundabout housed an enormous model of Sinbad the sailor's boat. Our first sight of the building took our breath away – it had wonderful Islamic architecture with a gold-topped dome glinting in the sun. In front of the equally impressive gold entrance stood two doormen, magnificently attired in traditional white costume and bearing, in front of their waists, the wonderful 'Khunjars', which are traditional beautifully-curved daggers, housed in exquisitely decorated sheaths. These khunjars are unique to Oman. Our daughter had reserved a beautiful 'Arabian' suite for us – this was an anniversary to remember! Our room had a balcony overlooking the beautiful bay; inside the hotel the Islamic architecture and pure opulence was to be admired, and outside we had the beautiful blue sea and a pure white beach, all fringed by verdant green coconut palms.

This was the first of several wonderful holidays in this fascinating country. Sue would pack a picnic (I have memories of cheese sandwiches, fruit, crisps and lots of water), we would get into her 4X4 (which she loved), and off we would set. Sometimes it would be to one of the numerous 'wadis' – I remember one called Wadi Shab, which was prone to flash floods. Another time it would be to ascend Jebel Akhdar, which at 3000 metres gave fantastic views and you really felt you were alone, and on top of the world. That is, until a local tribesman (they were shepherds known as Shawawi) appeared from nowhere trying to sell you a handwoven rug! We watched fishermen at the coast landing their catch and were amazed at the still-practised craft of hand-building dhows, some exceptionally large, as they had done for centuries.

We visited the old, restored city of Nizwah, and again, ancient crafts were very visible – wonderful doors and intricately painted and carved ceilings. Nizwah was formerly the capital of Oman. I can remember us visiting one of the wadis and climbing high above it; it was quite bare and rocky, and we came upon an area which looked down on a wonderful pool of clear turquoise water. I think the drop must have been about 200 metres. Not perturbed, our daughter asked her dad to join her in a dive, which he did. Another such occasion involved an underground swim which seemed to lead from one chamber to another. Needless to say, I took part in neither of these activities!

Our holiday ended at the beginning of the following year, but not before we attended the wonderful New Year's Eve dinner dance at the Naval Club. It was, as was the custom years ago, formal dress, with the men attired in their dinner suits and bow ties. I will never forget David, dressed immaculately, cycling alongside us as we walked to the club, but cycling with a difference – on his monocycle! We had a wonderful night to bring our holiday to a close.

Back to the UK

Our return to the UK almost never happened, as, due to the Gulf War our flight was cancelled. Sue and David went to the airport and finally succeeded in getting us on another flight which went to London. Our departure was delayed by a day, but we were not grumbling. We got back to a cold January in the UK, but rather than drive straight back to Wales we called to Cheltenham to see our son, his wife and our much-loved grandson, Nicholas.

Back in Wales, we had our last few months in our Baglan house and just before Easter we moved to Carmarthenshire. It was, initially, a small close of detached houses, and we were led to believe that development had finished – sadly, this turned out to be untrue. It was, however, a spacious four-bedroomed house with a pleasant, manageable garden at the rear of which ran a woodland stream. There were pleasant neighbours and we settled in very quickly – this was a necessity, as a few days later we were flying out to Cyprus, to move into our renovated village home. The sale of our Baglan property had financed the work that had been done and allowed us to be able to furnish it.

During recent months, my father's health had deteriorated. I called to my parents' house every day after work and my father spent three days a week at Tonna Hospital, which was, at that time, a specialist Alzheimer's hospital. Sometimes I would wait until the ambulance brought him home – I can remember his smiling face when he got off the vehicle. My father was always smiling, so whether the smile was habit or in recognition of me, I never knew, but I would listen to his replies on asking what he had done in Tonna and realise that I had lost him. My father was there in body, but the real man had disappeared. It was increasingly difficult for my mother as he was always trying to get out of the house, often in the middle of the night, and her role changed from being wife and companion to carer and warden, having to keep all doors locked and the keys with her.

Back to Cyprus, Easter 1992

We had arranged for a hire car to be waiting for us at the airport, and I can remember how excited we were at the prospect of seeing our new home. But when we arrived there in the late afternoon, we were SO disappointed! Rather than a lovely, renovated property, we were greeted with a 'work in progress'. We managed to find somewhere in the village to stay that night and the following morning addressed the situation with our builder, Hassan. He tried hard to charm his way into our hearts. There were many excuses and he said, 'I can find you a lovely house in the village' – to which our replies were 'Hassan, we HAVE a lovely house in the village, we are staying here'.

At this stage the bathroom was a mere shell, there was no staircase and the kitchen was unfinished. Undaunted, we managed to borrow an inflatable bed, and using some bedding we had brought, set up our 'camping' accommodation in the lounge – which at least had an entrance/ exit already completed, and the fireplace was finished.

What a holiday it proved to be! For the first two days we had to wash and toilet in the Crow's Nest. We watched whilst the carpenters finished fitting the pine kitchen units; one of them created and assembled the spiral staircase in front of our eyes. Finally, the electrical work was completed, the new cooker and washing machine were delivered, and we had functioning plumbing. Then came the task of buying furniture, and whilst we were doing this the garden, entrance patio and front gate were completed. By the time we had cleaned, shopped and established it as 'home' it was time to leave, but not before we visited one of the many ironworkers in Girne (Kyrenia) and had the name of the house beautifully crafted in wrought iron. We named it 'Eldoret', as it truly was the closest we came to living in Kenya.

That year continued without any great change. We delayed our visit to Cyprus that summer as Sue was coming over with David. After their departure we again flew over there and this time, after arranging for my father to stay in Tonna for two weeks, we took my mother with us for a break. She loved every minute of the holiday. We had some lovely evenings out – she particularly enjoyed eating at the Levante. We took her to a variety of beaches and she thoroughly enjoyed the warm, clear, Mediterranean Sea. I remember her remarking, as we drove away from one of the beaches, 'I can see you living here'. Unknown to us at that time, she was correct, and we spent many happy years as residents of that lovely island.

In 1992 John lost his remaining parent. His mother was a bit of a 'miracle,' as over 20 years previously she had been diagnosed with breast cancer. It was advanced and they performed a radical mastectomy, after which she received radiotherapy. She had also had some lymph glands removed. The treatment was harsh, and in those days the after-effects of radiotherapy were not good, but it saved her life. I remember visiting her in the old Port Talbot hospital; there were four women in her ward, and all had received the same treatment for breast cancer. Sadly, we later discovered that she was the only one of the four who had survived, but the cancer had now recurred in her remaining breast and was advanced. Her health deteriorated and she was now living with her daughter, Hilary, who looked after her very well. She remained in bed most of the time and they had brought the bed into the living room so that she was not isolated. On the first of February we received the phone call from Hilary – her mother had passed away.

On my side of the family things were now difficult, and it was time for my father to go into care, as looking after him was getting impossible for my mother. Initially we had tried to place him in a nursing home; my mother seemed reluctant to admit that my father, as he was, had gone. I remember I had the job of taking him in. I broke my heart after leaving him; sadly, although the real characters of Alzheimer's patients have disappeared, their relatives feel so much guilt when they must take them into care.

The following morning, my mother received a phone call to say that the home could not cope with him. John and I collected him and took him home to my mother. I contacted Tonna Hospital, where he went for day care and where he had stayed when my mother came to Cyprus. I explained the situation, and, within a few days, he was given a place there. It really was heart-breaking. Even though he was in a different place, mentally he was still our lovely husband, father and grandfather.

My mother visited almost every day. I went at least three times a week and often in between we would call to see him on our way home from college. On a weekend I would often take him for a car-ride, but he was always anxious to get back to what he now called 'home' – the hospital. The staff were wonderful; if there was a birthday, the residents would be treated to a wonderful 'party' with plenty of food and lots of music – most of them loved singing. When he had a particularly bad day, I would drive home with tears pouring down my face. On other days we could smile and laugh; sometimes when I visited, I would not be able to find him, because he had wandered to another room and would be sleeping on someone else's bed!

The worst experience we had was when, much later and after my mother's death, we received a phone call from Tonna asking us to go there immediately My father, the gentlest. kindest man you could wish to meet, had become violent – it was a terrible sight. He was like a frightened animal that was being attacked – the nurses could not go near him. I was so upset to see him like that. John tried gently talking to him. Initially my father was abusive, but finally he calmed down, and we had to sign the form 'sectioning' him so that they were able to give him the necessary injection to calm him. It was a horrible experience, and so sad, to see someone's personality change so completely.

The hospital was divided into three bungalows. Initially my father was in the first, then, as he deteriorated, he was transferred to the second. I just prayed that he would die before he was put in the third, as most of the patients there were completely bed-ridden and often incapable of feeding themselves etc. One thing never changed – his lovely smile and our love for him.

Sue continued in Oman, but her friendship with David had ended. He was transferred to Norway. Sue sold his yacht and also went to Norway, but the distance between them was a barrier, although they always remained friends. Nigel and Judith increased their family; our one and only granddaughter, Lauren Emily, was born in Cheltenham in October 1992 and we were overjoyed. When the time came for christening, Nigel and Judith brought her to Wales and she was christened in our local church.

Once living on this lovely island we soon got used to the change in customs and naturally, adapted ourselves to accept them. Like Africa, there were strict 'rites de passage'. In Africa it meant young men making their first kill; for women it was the painful removal of the clitoris. Young women would be taken to a particular spot where there would be cold running streams: in this icy water they would sit in in order to lessen the pain while a female witch doctor performed the clitorodectomy. In North Cyprus it was the ceremony of circumcision for boys. Not long after we lived there we witnessed a young boy riding on a donkey which was led by, I assume, his father. The boy was dressed in pale blue satin with a matching hat. Behind the donkey there was a long procession of people, obviously family and friends who had been invited to witness the event. The young boy was smiling - hard to believe when you think of the pain he was going to endure! Apparently a hall would be rented for the occasion and the young boy would lie down in front of his audience whilst the ceremony was performed. Afterwards the guests would walk up to him and leave money, either pinned to his clothing or alongside him, and congratulate him on reaching manhood. We in Western culture find these practices abhorrent, but it is part of their culture, even if we feel they are barbaric. Strangely, neither of these painful processes exhibit pain felt by the participants, and I wonder if they make people more stoic and able to endure pain in later life?

Cyprus was to become our 'escape', a place where we could just relax and build up our resources before going back. I remember collecting Nicholas and taking him, plus my aunt and uncle, out to Cyprus at Easter 1993. The island is particularly beautiful in spring: the almond trees are usually still in bloom, and the pink of their blossom against the verdant greenery is a sight to behold: the hills are awash with wild flowers. They include beautiful red anemones, which are often mistaken for poppies; bright yellow chrysanths and buttercups; geraniums and cyclamen, and the tall, magnificent wild fennel which grows in abundance, its bright yellow flowers covering the hillside. This is not to mention the early blossoming bougainvillea and the many species of beautiful wild orchids. It was on this holiday that Nicholas had his first experience of picking an orange from a tree.

CHAPTER 6

My mother's illness, and more travels

Later that year I had some health problems, but looking back, I think they may have been stress related. I was home from college with ill health when I received a phone call from my mother's next-door neighbour. She told me that she was concerned about my mother as she had a 'strange colour'. I immediately rang my mother and she said she had not been feeling too good. I made an appointment in her surgery, drove from Carmarthenshire to Baglan and took her for the appointment. I cannot remember what the doctor said, but I think he gave her medication, and I took her home.

After settling her in, I went home, saying I would come back the following morning. This I did and saw immediately that she was quite ill. She looked terrible, her skin was yellow, and she was so weak. I immediately phoned the doctor and said it was an emergency. The same doctor who had seen her the previous day arrived and on examination he turned to me and said 'how didn't I notice her skin colour yesterday?' He rang the hospital and told me to take my mother in. This I did, stayed to settle her in and visited that evening. Strangely, she looked happy to be in hospital and I left her smiling.

The following night when John and I visited, I was asked to speak to the doctor; investigations had shown that my mother had pancreatic cancer. I was shocked and distraught, and said nothing to her. The following day I was with her when she was told – and told that it was terminal. She had already guessed, because prior to marriage she had been a nurse. I prepared her bedroom and the next day I took her home to Carmarthenshire, to live with us. I always found it strange that my mother, who had always taken great pride in her home, never asked about her Baglan house after that and regarded our home as her home.

Initially, things were not too bad. Some days were better than others. She was registered with our GP, who was fantastic with her. A smart woman who took a pride in her appearance, she loved it when the doctor complimented her and said how smart she looked. I used to drive her to a local hairdresser – she loved having her hair done! Then she started deteriorating. I was now taking her to Singleton Hospital, and she was told about chemotherapy. I spoke to our GP and we both felt that in her present state of health the treatment was not a good idea. By this time, I had retired on health grounds.

My mother got weaker and weaker. I would tempt her with certain things and then she would have a yearning for a particular food, which I would provide. She was spending more and more time in bed, as she was so weak. This was the time when Lauren was going to be christened from our house. I remember I was in the kitchen ironing the starched, long christening gown in readiness for the Sunday when the phone rang – it was Singleton Hospital asking for my mother to go to start chemotherapy. I went upstairs and tried to dissuade her, using the christening as a reason for her not to go. She was adamant and said, 'I have to try, Helena'. I took her and with a heavy heart, watched as she was spoken to by one of the doctors, who was explaining the treatment to her. I can never forgive that man. He asked if there were any questions, and my mother said, 'will I be able to look after myself, do my housework, shopping etc?' His response 'of course'. I went with her to the small ward and left, saying I would be back that evening. All day I worried, determined I would stop her having that treatment – she was too weak. But it was futile. By the time I got back she was already on the drip receiving the chemotherapy.

The next few weeks were a nightmare. My mother got weaker and weaker, and I slept every night in the hospital. On the day of the christening Judith and Nigel had taken Lauren in her gown to visit my mother before the service. It was to be the only time she would see her great granddaughter, and the last time she would see Nicholas. She was desperately ill and the fact that I was sleeping and part-living in the hospital, did not do me much good. I can remember, on one occasion, when I bent over to give her a kiss, she said, 'why do we leave it so late to tell someone that we love them?' She was not an affectionate person, and sadly, that is the only time in my life that I can remember my mother saying she loved me.

She knew she was dying, and she wanted to die at home. I saw the specialist (he was Polish, I seem to remember). He refused, and told me that if I took her home, I would be killing her. She begged again to come home, and I told them that I wanted an ambulance to take her. I rang John and he brought a bed into our lounge and by some means fixed a wire coat hanger to the curtain rail behind the bed so that her drip could be fixed. One of my mother's brothers, Roy, who had been so supportive, came to the hospital, and with the drip in situ, we travelled in the ambulance, which drove slowly and carefully to our home.

That night was the most horrific I have ever had. I sat with my mother, moistening her dry mouth regularly, holding her hand and just trying to keep her comfortable. At 9 pm a district nurse called; by this time my mother had a terrific temperature. The nurse phoned our GP, who told her to take the drip down. Whether he thought that would hasten the end, I do not know, but I sat at her side all night, listening to the terrible sounds she was making. She seemed unconscious, but I kept swabbing her dry mouth and at 7 am she heaved her last sigh and passed away. It was an horrific and heart-breaking experience.

The following day I had to go to Tonna and try to tell my father. I took him aside and, with John alongside me, we told him that Mum had died. He immediately started crying, wailing. A nurse came along and asked him what the matter was, and he replied, 'My father has died'. From that day I became, in his eyes, my mother, and he spoke to me as if I were her. At first, when grieving, it hurt me, but later I was glad that I could, in some way, be a comfort to him.

Now really in need of a break, we were glad to have the village house in Karmi to go to. With promises from Roy, my mother's brother, and May, her sister, that they would visit my father, we flew to Cyprus and spent a wonderful week there. I needed to recharge my batteries, and I felt so much stronger returning home.

Oman again

At Christmas, we again flew to Oman and met Dan, who was later to become Sue's husband. He was a graduate, from Warwick, but was not using his degree, preferring instead to work for his brother Tim, who had a landscaping/pool business in Oman. We also met Dan's parents, who were staying with his brother and family. Tim and his wife Marion gave us a warm welcome and I remember having a lovely Christmas day with them and their two daughters.

Sue had moved out of the Shell apartment and she and Dan had rented a very nice house. She seemed very happy, and as long as she was happy, so were we.

Again we explored Oman. One wonderful weekend Dan's parents, his sister Pippa and ourselves were taken for a wonderful trip to Ras al Hadd nature reserve, and we camped that night in a small, beautiful bay called Raz al Jinz . Sue and Dan had organised it all, and we were truly spoilt. I remember taking a trip out on the bay with a local fisherman, bathing in the clear waters and then having a fantastic barbecue. The following morning, we were treated to a full English breakfast, but in BBQ style.

I loved visiting the Souk in Muttrah – also Muttrah itself, with its really striking white Portuguese architecture. I found the falaj canal system fascinating. I also enjoyed the thrills of driving up and down the dunes in Wahiba sands, and admired the magnificent opulence of the marble-clad Sultan Qaboos mosque. Oman is certainly a fascinating and beautiful country.

Back home Nigel and Judith had bought a lovely cottage in the Northamptonshire village of Welton. We visited, but I also had to regularly visit my father, whose health was deteriorating. Many years before, he had had a pacemaker fitted, but the doctor in Tonna, a very caring man, told me that his heart was not performing well. When I took him for a walk in the grounds he would get very breathless. Sometimes I would drive to our house so that he could spend the afternoon there – he usually slept for the whole time. By June, he was virtually bedridden, and I started sleeping at the hospital. Sadly, the pacemaker he had had fitted years previously was keeping him alive, when he deserved to die in peace – it was cruel. I pleaded with the doctor who was there (his usual doctor was away) to remove the pacemaker and give him release, but at that time, they were not allowed to do this. It was like some sort of horror film – his body deteriorating but his heart beating. Eventually, he passed away and was laid to rest with my mother; they died within a year of each other.

John, by this time, had been offered the chance of early retirement. Due to our recent family experiences, we were fully aware that life passes by too quickly, so he accepted the offer, and by September 1994 we were both retired.

Back to Africa

I had a desperate longing to go back to Africa, and we had seen a 'small ship' cruise advertised where you flew to Mombasa, joined the ship, and cruised down the coast of Africa, ending in Cape Town and then flying home. As John had now taken early retirement, we decided this was the time. It sounded a wonderful trip. The ship was advertised as having 'polished wooden decking, gleaming brass, a beautiful swimming pool'. Reality? Holes in the decking, rusty brass and a leaking pool. When we were shown into our cabin we insisted on being moved – the AC over the bed was leaking and the bedding was wet!

Despite the quality of the ship, which all the approximately fifty passengers complained about, we had lovely company. The food was appalling, and the 'afternoon tea', which one would expect to be of a certain standard, was served at one end of the deck, not indoors. It consisted of a tea urn full of water, some sachets of assorted teas, thick white china mugs, and some sandwiches and cakes left out so that the flies could land on them! We all, in turn, had the most horrific sickness/diarrhoea, some people being extremely ill. Despite this, we visited some fantastic places and made the most of the holiday. I must add that after our return a group of us collectively took the firm to court and recouped a large proportion of the cost of the cruise.

The journey was so interesting. We visited Zanzibar, saw the horrific prison where the slaves had been kept; had coffee in the square where they had erected a statue to their most famous inhabitant, Freddie Mercury, and travelled to a spice farm, where the fragrance as you approached was beautiful. There we met some lovely African children and young people. Our next stop was Mozambique, which had, of course, been wrecked by war. It was so poor and there were remnants of buildings which stood out to remind you of the horrors of war, but the coastline was superb, and I believe some Europeans were starting to buy land and build beach houses there. We made several stops on the coast of South Africa and visited Durban – which we were not too keen on, as it had a lot of crime. One small town which impressed us was Mossel Bay, and this was not just because it was a pleasant town situated on the coast, but because there was no obvious evidence of apartheid – black and white people mingled together in the shopping precinct. Cape Town was beautiful, and we were SO relieved to be able to go into one of the lovely restaurants on the harbour and have a decent meal!

We ascended Table Mountain and took a trip to see the penguins on the beach. We also visited the lovely botanical gardens there and admired the nearby road of rainbow-like coloured houses. A coach took us to visit the Khoisan tribe – they make a peculiar 'throaty' sound when chanting and this is the tribe of Nelson Mandela. It was, to say the least, a 'tourist' attraction, with a brie served for our meal. This was followed by tribal dancing and then the expected gratuities – very commercially orientated, but still interesting.

Life in Cyprus

Our holidays in Cyprus continued and we made many friends there. Often my mother's sister May and her lovely husband Dan would visit for a few weeks, and we also took our grandson Nicholas with us. Our next-door neighbour was Sir Michael Graydon, former equerry to the Queen and Air Chief Marshal of the Royal Air Force. He, and several other squadron leaders had been stationed in southern Cyprus in the 1960s and I believe he was one of the first to lease a Karmi property in around 1969.

We explored the island, visiting Kantara Castle and walking up to St. Hilarion Castle, where reputedly Richard III had stayed. The views from there were fantastic! I remember taking Nicholas up there and he marvelled at the birds flying below. In the summer, visits to Lefkosa (Nicosia), the capital, were made early in the morning, as later in the day it was too hot. I loved the market there – apparently it has now been replaced by a new one – but the one I remember was fascinating, selling everything from oranges and artichokes to fresh spices and Turkish tea. There was a restaurant that served delicious Turkish lentil soup and good pides (Turkish pizza). I can remember them starting to renovate the Buyuk Han (the great/big Inn), commonly referred to as Caravanserai. What a magnificent building! A central courtyard housing a lovely fountain, flanked by magnificent arched colonnades. The lower rooms had been used as shops, whereas the upper floor housed the accommodation where travellers could rest.

We made visits to Famagusta, flanked by its wonderful Venetian walls, the gated entrance with its iron door, and the mosque, which was originally a 14th century Gothic cathedral. Just outside the city is the ancient city of Salamis, which is totally unspoilt. From so many places in Cyprus you have wonderful coastal views: just outside Girne is the beautiful Bellapais Abbey, which allows breath-taking views, whilst the abbey itself seems to instil a sense of peace and calm to its visitors. A year or two before we left the island, they started to have classical concerts there and it proved to be the perfect setting. The 14th century Kyrenia castle is also a fascinating building, and I seem to remember it housed the oldest recovered shipwreck, from about 300 BC. Later, before we left the island, they used to host wonderful concerts and plays in the central courtyard.

Apart from all the fascinating history there were wonderful forest and mountain walks, and one must not forget the lovely beaches. Often, with friends or just on our own, we would travel to the Karpas, visit the Apostolos Andreas monastery and stay at the Blue Seas hotel. This was situated in a small cove north of the magnificent six kilometres of white sands. The hotel was basic, but we loved it. It really was like escaping from the world, and all you could hear was the gentle lapping of the warm sea. The only other noise was early in the morning – you might awaken to the sound of the proprietor's boat leaving the small harbour when he went out to fish. You would certainly NOT burn the midnight oil here, as the generator went off at 10 pm – there was no mains electricity. I can remember sitting outside on the balcony at breakfast and watching dolphins as they leapt out of the sea when passing by. Dinner would be whatever fish had been caught that day, all beautifully served with a delicious salad served in a dressing that only Mediterranean people seem to be able to make. This was always followed by wonderful fresh fruit, which really DID taste fresh, as if it had just been collected. The Karpaz also boasted wild donkeys and shepherds and, at the due date, turtles hatching their eggs.

CHAPTER 7

Fire, and moving to Cyprus

It was while we were on one of our visits to Karmi, when my aunt and uncle had come to stay, that we witnessed the horrific fire of1995. It was the 27th of June, our grandson Nicholas' birthday, and we were having a lazy afternoon swimming and relaxing on the beach. We had, by this time, decided that we were going to become permanent residents of Northern Cyprus and had sold our house in Wales, with the plan of buying land and building a house in Cyprus of our own design. On that day we had an appointment with an estate agent to look at a plot of land in the village of Ilgaz, which was the next village to Karmi, and one we often visited.

As we drove up to Ilgaz we saw flames on the mountainside and my aunt, extremely nervous, wanted to turn back. We saw one of the residents who lived below the village come out and douse himself with water. He said, 'there's a fire, I am going to see if I can put it out'.

Foolishly, we continued to climb up to the village. When we arrived, we could see that the fire was worse than we thought, but at this stage it was mainly to the right of the Ilgaz. We saw the plot of land and there was no sign of the vendor, so we rapidly got in the car and started to descend. I remember that when John and I got out of our vehicle, the wind almost ripped off the doors – it was horrific! The drive down the mountain was frightening, the wind had increased and was driving the massive flames over towards Karmi – I remember seeing them literally leap across the tarmac road from one side to the other.

Miraculously, our car was not caught in the ambush, and we sped back to our house. As we drove along the main road the mountainside was crimson with leaping flames, the fire had swept over towards our village. When we got home, John rushed to the pub and told people what was happening, and it was decided to evacuate the village. I quickly went into our house and rang our grandson, Nicholas, to wish him a happy birthday, and I can remember telling Judith 'the mountain is on fire and we are being evacuated!'

A few stalwarts, including Tony from the shop and Steve from the pub, decided, possibly foolishly, to remain. Not knowing where to go, we rapidly collected some basic needs and drove down the mountainside. We decided to go to the Jasmine Court Hotel, from where we could view the village and surrounding mountainside. I will never forget the generosity of that hotel, as they accommodated as many evacuees as they could and the next morning would take no money for our stay.

It was a terrible night. We watched the flames cover the entire mountainside; we had already found a buyer for our village property and obviously thought all was lost. The next morning, leaving my aunt and uncle in the hotel, John and I drove up towards Karmi. Everywhere was black, destroyed, trees still smouldering, smoke everywhere and the air smelt of destruction. As we approached nearer the village we gasped in amazement -practically all the Karmi houses were standing, intact! Only a few on the outskirts had been destroyed – the rampant, ferocious flames had leapt over the village and then continued over the mountainside. We could not believe our eyes, and we were so relieved and happy! Our house was intact. It just smelt of ash and fire and was covered in grey dust and particles.

A day of cleaning and we were back to normal, but the beautiful countryside was the victim of a holocaust, and it would take months for the vegetation to return and years for the beautiful pine forests to regrow. I can remember that for months afterwards, you would see the grey ashen remains of a tree suddenly alight with flames – the roots, deep under the earth, were still smouldering.

After that, my aunt never returned to Cyprus. We returned to the UK to finalise our affairs there and, having sold 'Eldoret' we rented another village house for a year, whilst we supervised the building of our new property. Just after the fire we bought a large plot of land on the mountainside below Karmi – we must have been the only people to love a blackened, scorched piece of ground, but it had wonderful views of the village in one direction and overlooked the Mediterranean from the front.

Realising we would need to buy a car for use on the island, when we returned to the UK, we sold both vehicles that we had there, and bought a car which was large enough for us to transport all our clothing and so on. We bought a vehicle which afforded space by the back seat being lowered, thus making it a virtual estate car. I persuaded John that we should make the journey a memorable one and drive out to Cyprus, which we did.

Driving to Kyrenia

I remember planning the route: we travelled down to Kent, stayed with my cousin Yvonne in her lovely oast house, then took the ferry across to the Continent and travelled down through Belgium, Switzerland and Italy, ending up at Brindisi. We had wanted to travel via Yugoslavia, which would have been more direct, but at that time there was a war there, so we had to take the route through Switzerland. I made a video of the whole journey -unfortunately now lost. The trip was so enjoyable, with stops en route. John had never seen the Swiss Alps and we had never visited the Italian lakes or been to Venice. On this trip, we were able to do all this. We stopped at Lasize, Lake Garda, Lake Como and Venice. I remember John saying that the spaghetti he had at Lake Garda was the best he had ever had. We found Venice beautiful, but crowded, expensive and commercialised – perhaps September was the wrong time to visit.

We got to Brindisi and boarded the ferry – this was just a 'means to an end' not, in any way, a cruise. After landing in Turkey at a port called Cesme, we stayed the first night at a hotel not far outside the town before starting our 560-mile journey to Tasucu the next day. The weather in Europe had not been good, but in Turkey it was sunny and warm – wonderful!

The journey was scenic and interesting. We drove along what

I believe is tagged the 'Turkish Riviera', and though our journey did not include stops at all the lovely places we passed – Kusadasi, Marmaris, Bodrum, etc – it was a truly scenic route, and I am so glad we did it. We were amazed at some of the lorries we saw. They were certainly overloaded, and we made sure that there was always a fair distance between us, as some of the cargoes were rather precariously placed.

One of the nicest meals (or so it seems) that I can ever remember having was on this journey. I remember us going round a bend in the road and coming upon a small bay. Before us lay the calm, turquoise water, and it was so peaceful. Opposite the little cove was a small building with an outside seating area which, if I remember, was covered by some sort of tarpaulin. It was a 'lokanta', a restaurant, and we stopped to have a late lunch. We were the only customers and the owner, a very friendly chap, brought us cold beers and then a large platter on which was displayed a variety of fish. He pointed to the small boat which was sitting in the small cove and we gathered that he had caught the fish that morning. We chose, he cooked, and he soon presented us with a delicious meal of freshly caught and barbecued fish, crisp French fries and a delicious salad. After this feast, he presented us with a platter of fresh fruit. I shall never forget it – sitting overlooking a turquoise, peaceful sea, with only us and the owner to disturb the silence. It is not opulence that brings the most happiness, it is those magical moments that are captured in your heart and remain there forever.

Leaving that lovely haven, we drove through Antalya (terribly busy) and then Alanya, and finally reached the pretty cobbled town of Silifke, which led us to the port of Cesme, where the final part of our journey would begin. It was now early evening, and the ferry was shortly to depart – alas, they said initially that it was about to leave and was full. I was almost in tears! However, after much pleading and much discussion, we were allowed to board. It was an overnight crossing, but we had no cabin. The ship was more than a little tired and we wondered if we would ever get to Kyrenia harbour. We later heard (I do not know if it was true) that the ship had been sunk in the last war and retrieved to be used as the ferry. We were rather apprehensive, and I remember neither of us being able to sleep. It was hot, stuffy and overcrowded. There were babies who, as is the Turkish custom, were wrapped up from head to toe and with the heat, were constantly crying. Lots of passengers were being sick, and one of the crew walked around with paper bags for people to use – it was the worst boat trip I have ever taken!

Early the next morning we arrived to the welcome sight of Kyrenia harbour, the yellow stone of its lovely castle glinting in the early morning sun. I have never been so glad to put my feet on terra firma.

Early years in Cyprus

Life continued. We supervised the building of our house and pool, moved in and loved our new abode. When I was at the kitchen sink, I was looking out at our swimming pool and beyond that the blue Mediterranean, and the same view could be seen from the bedrooms and lounge. Having spent a winter on the island, we realised that the winter months at altitude could be very cold, so we had central heating installed in addition to a lovely log fire. Life continued, but with one hiccup during the first few months. I was anxious to get our garden established and during our first winter was busy digging and planting, but on finishing I took off my wellington boots and damaged my spine. This meant that eventually I had to fly to the UK for major back surgery.

Our life continued to be kind to us: lots of friends, an active social life, and I became virtually in unpaid employment for two years as I was elected as Chairperson of the British Residents Society. Whilst in this role I made quite a few changes to the constitution, which was rather out-dated and very male orientated. It was hard work: sometimes I would get a phone call in the middle of the night from some elderly Brit requiring help or hospitalisation, repatriating someone who was elderly and unable to cope on their own, or getting involved with the needs of Turkish Cypriots – I started an annual charity ball (which I believe may still take place), the proceeds of which went to buy much-needed equipment for Girne (Kyrenia) hospital. With the help particularly of one of the committee members, Tony Hutchinson, we organised a blood donor day, as Turkish Cypriots suffer from the inherited blood disorder thalassemia, and blood was always in short supply.

I met so many interesting older British characters and remember them well, but sadly, I have forgotten some of the names! There was one who could tell you of her escape from Singapore during the war and being in a camp. Another lady, of Russian origin, had fled with her parents from Russia during the revolution and went to Germany; they had to flee Germany during Hitler's reign and then escaped to live in North Cyprus, where they experienced the 1974 war. Bill Dreghorn, who lived on the island for many years and wrote many articles and books on the historical aspects of the island, he was always very complimentary toward me and I really appreciated that.

There were many, many more. The danger of living in such a small part of an island is that you meet people you would not normally meet ie, in social class terms, and I was always careful to remember that. Unfortunately, some people did not, and started behaving as though they had been honoured by the Queen or were members of the aristocracy! An example of people I would not have met in the UK is Mike Graydon. Another example was Sir Edward and Lady Ashmore – though I must admit, he was the sweetest man, and I was so fond of them both. We went to their lovely small house on the mountain and there was always a warm welcome, but I would not have met the First Lord of the Admiralty in the UK!

I am in no way inferring that these people were any better than us, merely that in a country like Britain there is still a certain amount of class segregation, and the fact that this was dispelled on a small island was good.

A great friend of ours who was a perfect gentleman and a visitor to our home was Salih Dayioglu, who was, at that time, President of the Supreme Court. When I was looking for raffle prizes for the ball, Salih kindly introduced me to some of the biggest businessmen on the island, ensuring we had wonderful prizes, eg hotel breaks, airline return tickets to the UK etc, and were thus able to raise more money for the hospital. I remember one of my uncles, Uncle Roy, flew over to spend Christmas with us. Roy was a Justice of the Peace and when he knew this, Salih invited us to meet him for lunch in Lefkosa (Nicosia). Roy enjoyed chatting to him about the legal system in Cyprus and Salih took him on a guided tour of the courts.

Those nine years went by very quickly. For the school holidays I used to get a flight to Stanstead, disembark, meet my daughter-in-law for a coffee, then re-embark on the same plane with Nicholas and Lauren and take them back to Cyprus with me! They loved being there. We had a swimming pool and they just lived in it. John would spend hours teaching Nicholas to dive, and Nicholas, in turn, would teach Lauren to have the confidence to jump in the pool. Trips to the beach, the Karpaz, etc – lovely holidays. What became a ritual was that at whatever time they arrived – it was usually nearing midnight – the lights would be switched on around the pool and in they would jump!

At the end of the school holidays Nigel and Judith (and later William) would come over for the last few weeks and then take the children home with them. One very eventful 'pool night' was on John's 60th birthday. I had invited lots of people, there were tables set out around the pool, I supplied plenty of food and drink and Linda Smith had made a lovely birthday cake. Later in the evening two of our dear friends, John and Margaret Chawner, decided they would throw John, fully clothed, in the pool – they did not bargain for my husband, who pulled them both in with him!

Life in Cyprus was good, but apart from having lots of friends, we made sure that we stayed close to family. Sue, by now, had finished her four years in Oman and Shell offered her another contract in Nigeria – she declined, as Nigeria was then in a very unstable state. Instead, she took a post in the British School, Bangkok; after a year she left there and firstly taught in the Purple Elephant nursery school, where the boys later went, and then eventually transferred to a post in Shrewsbury School, Bangkok, where she was incredibly happy.

I am jumping ahead. We made more visits to Sue and to the UK. Our children all visited us. Dan's parents had a small house in the south of the island, so they would often incorporate visiting both sides when they came over, but later Sue would sometimes come without Dan, but with our grandchildren and we would sometimes escort her to Istanbul when it was time for her to leave.

Yet again, I am jumping ahead of time.

1997 was a memorable year. In April, Judith gave birth to William, our third grandchild. A few months later, Sue rang from Thailand to say that she and Dan were going to marry that summer. Dan's mum had cancer and I think they were hoping to marry before she died, but sadly, she passed away a few weeks before the wedding. I obviously hoped that they would marry in Cyprus, from our home. We had a lovely church (St. Andrew's), there were good dressmakers to make the gown, and plenty of lovely venues for a reception. Unfortunately, Dan was adamant; he wanted them to marry in the UK. I was devastated – our only daughter, and the only time in our lives when we did not own a property in the UK! It was decided that Sue would fly to England and she was staying with Nigel and Judith. Sadly, I was not with my daughter when she chose her dress etc. but Judith represented me. John and I booked into a hotel not far away and went over. We arranged the church, the flowers and the reception, and although a small wedding, it was a perfect day. They were married in Welton Church, the village where Nigel and Judith lived.

When we got back to Cyprus, we decided that we MUST have a base in the UK. It would mean that we would have somewhere to stay when visiting family and would also be useful to Sue and Dan when they went over. Nigel started looking on our behalf and found a nice two-bedroomed apartment in a lovely village not far from them. We went over, viewed, and bought, and invested in an INCREDIBLY old car which we could use when there. Our two older grandchildren, Nicholas and Lauren, used to call the car 'Grandma's red machine'!

Our life in Cyprus continued to be very pleasant. I had a gardener, but also did some of the work myself. Our garden, in the wonderful Mediterranean climate, flourished and grew. We had palm trees, various shades of bougainvillea, various other flowers and shrubs, plus lemon and orange trees. It was a delight to have a gin and tonic with slices of freshly picked lemon! I also used to make lemon ice cream, which the grandchildren loved.

One day one of John's golfing friends, a German gentleman who lived at the top end of the village on the start of mountain road to Ilgaz, asked John for a lift to Guzelyurt, where the golf club was. John noticed one of the last remaining ruins nearby and made enquiries with tourism. 'Yes, it's available for lease,' we were told. Immediately John's mind was in overdrive. We both took a walk up there and surveyed the little of the house that was left. Basically, it was about a foot of walls and some very overgrown land, However, being situated at the very top edge of the village it had superb views. To the right you could see Kyrenia and the coastline going further towards the Karpaz, and to the left you were looking downwards along the coast to Lapta. The seed was planted, and we thought that this would be a superb opportunity for our daughter to own her first house.

Immediately John started drawing and designed a lovely two-bedroomed house with a lounge, kitchen/diner, small downstairs veranda and large upstairs roof terrace. We rang Sue in Thailand and chatted to her about it. Initially she was not keen, and we felt she was losing a huge opportunity. Later, after much persuasion by Dan, she agreed that it was a chance not to be missed. She came over, visited the site (we had previously sent photos etc.) and signed her agreement with Tourism.

We used the same Turkish Cypriot builder for Sue's project as we had used for our house – in reality, Sue's project was virtually building new as there was so little of the original house remaining. There would be constant liaison and phone calls with Sue and lots of photos of the progress taken. It really turned out to be a beautiful two-bedroomed property, with lovely slate floors and the traditional beamed/straw ceilings, and it had such magnificent views!

Cyprus life continued to be good, with visits from Nigel, Judith and of course, Sue. She loved the island and we had so many lovely walks. The golf club was at the other end of the island, just outside Guzelyurt, and we would often go down there for a game of golf. The situation was superb, the greens running alongside the blue Mediterranean. The small old clubhouse was adequate – you took your own beers and put them in the fridge provided. After the game, and having a beer, we would call to Jemal's restaurant for delicious fish and chips. Sue always enjoyed those days.

CHAPTER 8

Turkey, the Far East and Australia

A trip to Egirdir

In May 1996, we went, with other Karmi residents, on a trip to Egirdir, Turkey. It was our first 'inland' Turkish trip and was thoroughly enjoyable. We saw so many interesting locations, buildings and people. The lake at Egirdir was beautiful, as were the old castle and mosque. We visited the ancient ruins and the lovely market square at Yalvac, and I will never forget the market at Isparta, which seemed to go on for miles – I have never seen such a wonderful display of fresh vegetables and fruit. One of the highlights of the trip was to see the shimmering travertines of Pamukkale and the magnificent ruins and amphitheatre of Hierapolis. This ancient city dates back to 190 BC and is fascinating with ancient pillars, pools and stone paths, but the *pièce de résistance* is the magnificent amphitheatre – a sight not to be missed.

Life continued – full, but happy times. We visited the UK, visited Thailand and the family came over to us.

Thailand – and a grandson

Sue was now pregnant, and the baby was due the following spring. When she asked if we would go over for the birth, we did not need a second invitation! We got there a while before it was due and took the opportunity to do some sightseeing. We enjoyed travelling on the Bangkok rivers in a long-tailed boat, and John and I did the usual tours – the lovely Vimanmek Teak Palace, the beautiful Wat Arun (Temple of the Dawn), the night markets and the National Museum, etc. Eventually, a little overdue, the baby, Oliver Lloyd, made his appearance on 5th March by Caesarean section. He was long, tiny, and looked very tired – it had obviously been a huge effort trying to enter the world!

Sue came home, had some rest and then we all we went for a lovely break in Hua Hin. Sue had settled into the role of motherhood very easily, adored her son, and was now getting back to normal after a difficult birth.

Our route to Thailand involved a stop in Istanbul, and as the wait for connection was long, we often stayed overnight. I can honestly say that I think Istanbul is one of my favourite cities in the world. It has a magical atmosphere, being halfway between the East and West. Its location, on the shores of the Bosphorous, is wonderful, and it has such beautiful buildings and so much history. The beautiful Hagia Sophia, with its 6th century dome and Christian mosaics, is breathtaking. Then there is the magnificent Topkapi Palace towering high above the Bosphorous, and Dolmabahce Palace, where the famous Ataturk spent his last days. There is so much to see in this wonderful city which has been occupied through time by so many different powers, nationalities and religions, as reflected in its culture and architecture. The Romans, Egyptians, Byzantines and Christians have all left their signatures on this beautiful city.

Apart from history and architecture, Istanbul has wonderful old Turkish architecture with traditional Turkish houses, many of which are now hotels. There are rug sellers alongside Topkapi, and on the quayside fishermen sell newly barbecued tuna in chunks of fresh bread. Then there are the bazaars, such as the grand or 'buyuk' (big) bazaar, which is famous for its Turkish rugs – they say you get the best bargain first thing in the morning, as then you bring luck to the vendor for that day. Whether that is true, or not I hesitate to say, but I always fall for these superstitions! The common name 'buyuk' is indeed apt, as the bazaar is huge – I think about 30,000 square metres. My favourite was always the smaller, more intimate, but equally, or perhaps even more, intriguing, Egyptian Bazaar, more commonly known as the Spice Bazaar. Here the aromas of all the different herbs and spices are wonderful. There are various teas, oils, essences, Turkish delight, and honeycombs, apart from every spice you can think of. Istanbul boasts many more markets which thrive alongside the new, smart, shopping malls, but for me, the old bazaars are what makes the city so unique.

Time marched on and the next year Sue produced her second son; Ben was born in September 1999. Again, we were in Thailand for the birth and loved being there. Oliver was now the 'big brother'. Sue was in a lovely mother and baby group and had a lot of nice friends. She and Dan had a good social life, with the facilities of the British Club, Bangkok being well used. Children could have swimming lessons, families could meet, and good meals shared with friends. I think motherhood brought Sue and me closer together than ever. There had been a period when, both having strong views and ideas, we used to disagree, though nothing major and no disagreement ever stayed. I am grateful for the love and friendship we shared, and with the birth of the boys we were closer than ever.

Malaysia

Again, travel was inevitable. Every time we visited, Sue would beg us to stay longer by doing a 'visa' run, ie we would leave the country and then re-enter for a further stay. The year that Oliver was born this meant a trip to Malaysia and a stay in the capital, Kuala Lumpur. I loved Malaysia, as it exhibited a wonderful blend of the old and the new. We saw the Petronas twin towers, made of glass and steel, and I remember us ascending in the lift to the observation deck at the top – the lift seemed to literally fly to the top. The lovely old colonial buildings were still present – the railway station, the law courts, and the cricket ground/pavilion. We visited the Batu caves, which lie north of the capital and are the scene of that Hindu festival which takes place in January, where pilgrims pierce their skin, sometimes in the most painful way, and endure self-torture before ascending the 275 steps which lead to the top of the caves. I am proud to say that we managed the mammoth climb, a feat which I could certainly not do today!

Then there was the market, which was fascinating and sold everything you could think of, from cheap leather sandals to beautifully executed paintings. We also took a trip to a rubber plantation, where John tried his hand at extracting rubber from the tree, and finally, the Royal Pewter Company, where we could witness the making and decorating of various pewter items.

Exploring Thailand

Our many visits to Thailand meant that we travelled throughout the country, in addition to making 'visa runs' to various places.

Bangkok, like Kuala Lumpur, was a mixture of old and new, albeit without the traces of colonialism. On one occasion we visited Muang Boran (the ancient city), which is just outside Bangkok and well worth a visit. It encompasses the whole of Thailand's most famous monuments and buildings over a large 200-acre site. It was wonderful and allowed you to see buildings/temples which would otherwise have been impossible to see.

On one occasion John and I went to Chang Mai for a weekend. Up country Thailand is beautiful. In addition to seeing Chang Mai and experiencing its lovely night market, we took the opportunity of visiting the hill tribes – all very unspoilt and the women and children we met were delightful, beautifully dressed in their colourful attire. We rafted down the river and went elephant trekking – I fear I would not do the latter today as I hate elephants being used as tourist attractions. On this occasion, the mahut asked John if he would like to take over – what a disaster! The elephant, deciding he wanted a drink, bent over a stream, drank water and then, raising his trunk, decided that John should have a shower!

One of the most memorable, albeit upsetting trips we made was when Ben was a baby. We visited the famous River Kwai and saw what remained of the original bridge, walked over the new one and saw the engine that was used in the war. We had a beautiful hotel overlooking the famous river – I remember having a delicious meal on a floating restaurant there. That was the nice part, but the visit to Hell Fire Pass will stay in my memory for ever. The Japanese wanted to construct a railway between Burma and Thailand, and to do so they used Australian and British prisoners of war. The construction started simultaneously from Burma and Thailand in 1942. The excavation of sheer rock was carried out with the most primitive tools; the men toiled in extreme heat and some of the wettest monsoons seen for years. In these conditions they were forced to work for 12-18 hours at a time; if they wanted to leave for the purpose of relieving themselves, they were beaten. It truly was 'hell on earth', hence the name 'Hell Fire Pass'. Sixty-nine men were beaten to death by the guards, and many lost limbs. The famous Australian surgeon Sir Edward 'Weary' Dunlop worked tirelessly trying to save men's limbs, but often had to amputate – he and his colleagues would work night and day with the crudest of facilities. I remember seeing photographs of how they used bamboo to substitute the drip tubing that would normally be used in such situations. Gangrene, cholera, dysentery – how those poor men suffered. I can remember both Sue and me shedding tears – it truly epitomised 'man's inhumanity to man'.

After our visit here we went down river to Chungkai cemetery, where 1692 men are buried. Another moving moment, but I am glad we did that trip as we owe those men so much. It is true – we must never forget.

Another memorable trip made with the family and this time Gerry, Dan's father, was to the ancient city of Ayutha, the former capital of Siam, where we were treated to an archaeological treat of ancient temples, palaces and monasteries, some dating back to the 10th century. So much to see and wonder at. Thailand is far more than beaches and nightlife!

In saying that, I also have some memorable beach memories – spending New Year on Coral Island; Chalong Bay, near Phuket; Hua Hin with the lovely hotel restored from the old railway station... wonderful memories, only afforded us by our daughter's life abroad. Thailand was a time when Sue was so happy and so sad. She made many friends, all of whom became friends to us, and even though they are spread throughout the world, they keep in touch with me and for that I am so grateful. One attraction which is not quite the same – I used to love Chatuchak market at the weekend, but the last time I was in Bangkok it had moved further outside Bangkok and I felt that it had lost some of its wonderful atmosphere. It was a great place to view the produce of Thailand, from wood carvings to fish, plants to livestock, street food to restaurants, all in one place, albeit a huge area, and one usually ended feeling rather tired!

Burma

On 8th March 2001, Sue and Dan's third child arrived – the lovely Sam. Again, a visit was required and again we did a 'visa' trip. This time we flew somewhere I had always wanted to visit – Burma. Out of all our travels, I believe Burma was one place that fascinated me the most. Few visitors entered the country at this time, and there were strict rules regarding how much money you could take in etc. We were warned that some of the employees in the airport were not to be trusted regarding offers of currency exchange. One thing that stands out in my mind was the character of the Burmese people, who were kind, welcoming and gentle. It was, for us, like stepping back in time, but for the Burmese, life was hard and they had been through such a period of subjugation and unrest. Unfortunately things have not changed, and I feel such empathy for these lovely people.

Of course, it is no longer Burma but Myanmar, its capital no longer Rangoon but the similar Yangon. You cannot visit Yangon without experiencing the omnipresent Shwedagon golden stupa. The city itself was full of old, neglected but beautiful buildings, many of which were remnants of colonial Britain. Some had been renovated, or at least kept useable, and were now being altered for their new roles. The road system was (or at least had been, when it was maintained) superb, with wide streets, crossroads etc. I often wonder what would have happened to this country if the British had never occupied it. An extremely rich country, Burma has so many natural resources: jewels of all sorts, diamonds, emeralds, jade, sapphires, and rubies – Burmese rubies are reputed to be the best in the world. It is rich in minerals and has oil reserves and natural gas. Its forests have, unfortunately, been stripped of much of the teak, its natural valuable resource. Britain had been active in Burma since 1824, but it was in 1885 that Britain invaded and claimed Burma as part of its Indian nation, and the then King Thibaw was exiled to India, where he remained for the rest of his life. Sadly Burma, and its people, have been in a state of war and unrest ever since. The royal family had ruled the country for about one thousand years, I somehow think that if they had continued to rule, it would have remained at peace. The upper echelons of British society lived well in Burma – we were shown the remnants of the Governor's residence and it was enormous – much bigger than Buckingham Palace. We also visited the golf club there; it was rather rundown and in need of some TLC, but it was easy to visualise what it was like when Britain ruled.

Burma was as if time had passed it by: people still used ox carts and we visited a pot factory, where the women were making earthenware pots by hand, their powdered white faces still offering a smile as their feet turned the kiln. When I say factory, it was all done outdoors, not inside a building.

I can now honestly say that we travelled on the 'road to Mandalay' as we went, by ox cart, to visit the spectacular Chankhtatgyi reclining Buddha, resplendent in its gold covering and 66 metres long. The market in Yangon was fascinating, its people warm and welcoming and I would so love to visit this country again. It does not deserve all the unrest it has seen and continues to see during the present century.

Seeing the family

There were lots more family visits: us to the UK, the UK family to us, Sue, Dan and the boys to us and us to Thailand. All the grandchildren made really good use of the pool and Lauren could now dive in. On one occasion when Sue came on her own with the boys, I remember booking us into an Istanbul hotel for a few days when she was going back. We had a wonderful trip up the Bosphorous and a lovely lunch overlooking the water before returning downstream.

Amid all this happiness were two very sad occasions, or

should I say one sad and one tragic. The first was when Nigel and Judith's marriage broke up. We had known Judith since she was a teenager and she was the mother of our three grandchildren, but these things happen and there was nothing we could do about it. The second tragic occasion was when we received a phone call early in 2002 to tell us that Sue had been diagnosed with breast cancer. She was 37 years old. Friends in Cyprus rallied around, I can remember the Chawners offering to look after the house and pool.

We hurriedly booked our flights and left almost immediately. It was good to be of help and support to our wonderful daughter. After surgery and chemotherapy there followed radiotherapy and John took her every day. He miraculously managed to drive through the horrendous Bangkok traffic – there was no sky train at that time – and he said he would now be able to drive anywhere in the world, as nowhere could be worse than Bangkok!

Sue was positive and cheerful, and I was able to amuse the boys and somehow persuade my stubborn daughter to rest. I would pick them up from school, collect them from friends, manage to join in activities at Ben's gym club (a miracle) and hope that the treatment worked.

Perth, Australia

Again, we were persuaded to do a visa run and this time we visited Perth, Australia, where my young cousin Janet lived. Janet's eldest son, Brian, had visited Sue when she was in Oman and apparently had a great time. Sue had also spent time in Oz with Janet and her husband Brian. I remember what a warm welcome we had. Brian senior, Janet's husband, and her younger son

John, collected us form the airport – very unexpected as we had thought to get a taxi. Jan had a beautiful home just across the road from the beach in Scarborough, which is a suburb of Perth. The house had a super pool, and we would sit around there in the evenings, usually drinking more than we should, and I always remember John, Janet's youngest, acting as barman!

Young John seemed to get on very well with my husband John, and I remember my husband borrowing Janet's sports car to visit the off licence. Young John said that he would go with him to show him the way and on the way the younger John was urging the driver to go faster and faster – I think they both enjoyed the trip! Jan and Brian also had a house inland at the golf course – my husband loved it there and I had to talk him out of buying the house (it was for sale), as I think his love of golf was making him rather unrealistic!

We loved Perth. The old part was fascinating with the preserved Victorian buildings, and on Sunday there was a super indoor/outdoor market and everything was so clean. We hired a car and spent a few days driving down the coast, and were impressed. All so spacious, so clean, with plenty of parks and a lovely coastline. One thing that did not come up to our expectations was the hotels, which we thought were quite basic. We certainly regretted that we had not migrated years ago when an aunt of mine tried to persuade us to do so. On the other hand, would we have travelled to and lived in all the countries that we have? One must not, cannot regret what is past. Decisions are made at a certain time and they must always be the right decisions.

Life continued as normal, but John was tiring of Cyprus. I am not sure why, but he always, when living abroad, wanted to return to the UK. I'm not sure whether this was to do with his father's repeated insistence that 'the best country in the world is the UK'. Sue, Dan and the children came for a last visit, and even though they slept in their own house, our pool was well used! Dan wanted money to set up a new business and even though Sue had said she would never sell her Cyprus house – she maintained it was her anchor for wherever she lived – it was put on the market and it sold quickly. We also put our lovely home on the market and sold. The day we left I felt so sad; it reminded me of the day I last shut the gate on Ty'r Eglwys. Certain houses and locations have a special place in your heart.

As our only close family in the UK was Nigel, we bought a new house on the outskirts of Rugby, where he was living. Sue and family paid a visit, and it was lovely to see them, but I could not settle.

In 2005 we again flew to Thailand. It was Sue's 40th birthday and I had helped Dan to find a cottage to rent in Italy. Some were extortionately priced, but I managed to find a more reasonable one which Dan reserved. This was to be a complete surprise for Sue. We spent time over there before her birthday and she chose her present from us – an antique piece of Thai furniture. Her friend Julie organised a surprise party, and then Dan told her of the upcoming trip to Italy. I shall always remember how reluctant she was to leave her three boys, but she did, had a wonderful 40th and I thoroughly enjoyed looking after the boys with the aid of Sue's two wonderful maids, MuMu and Boontien.

Laos and Vietnam

Again, a visa run was necessary and this time we decided to visit Laos and Vietnam. Having never experienced a Thai rail journey, we thought this would be a good opportunity. I can remember us arriving at Bangkok railway station; it was chaotic, and I thought 'are we mad?' The experience, however, was great. We were beginning this trip by firstly visiting the Laos capital, Vientiane. The rail journey was disappointing in that you made most of the journey at night, so there were no countryside views. It was, however, a cheap and good way to travel, giving you Pullman experience at a fraction of the cost. One word of advice – eat before you board!

The following morning, we reached the Thai/Laos border. It was a short walk to the necessary border controls and then you could either get a tuk-tuk or taxi to Vientiane. The city itself was still very French, even though it was no longer a colony. There was not a lot to do in the city, but I remember the beautiful French architecture and so many lovely buildings in need of repair. The boulevards were wide and tree lined and we saw many Buddhist temples or shrines. I can also remember a central circular area which was surrounded by restaurants. We sat there one morning drinking wonderful coffee and eating delicious freshly made croissants, and felt as though we were in France.

From Vientiane we flew to Hanoi city, the capital of Vietnam, where we had already booked accommodation. It was a truly fascinating city, and there was much to see and do. Trying to cross the road was not for the faint hearted, for never in my life have I seen so many scooters! There were many graceful street vendors, carrying their wares in wooden or bamboo shoulder poles, with their wares filling the containers on each side – they seemed to have no problem balancing them. We strolled alongside the beautiful Hoan Kiem lake and went to the Municipal Water

Puppet Theatre, where we saw the expertise and craft of an art which has been practised in Vietnam for over a thousand years.

Not quite so beautiful, but still worth a visit, was the Hoa Lo French prison, formerly used to practise torture etc by the French. It was used during the last war to detain American POWs and is now commonly referred to as the 'Hanoi Hilton'. This was quite funny, as we were staying in the very centrally located and modern Hilton. Apparently, some of the POWs escaped from this prison by tunnelling through the very tiny sewers. Near our hotel – I seem to remember it was opposite – was the magnificent opera house, built by the French earlier this century.

The most significant and moving part of our visit was when we went to the Ho Chi Minh Mausoleum. Here there were crowds of people, but it was all very well managed and the people themselves acted with a reverent respect for the place, the embalmed body of Ho Chi Minh, and the life of this extraordinary man. We, like so many others, could walk past the open coffin wherein the embalmed body lay; no one could take in a camera, and it was all done with respect. We were then allowed to walk around the grounds and visit the small hut which was raised off the ground by bamboo poles – this is where Ho Chi Minh lived and wrote. He never, apparently, used the huge 'palace' but lived a simple life with few luxuries. It reminded me of Gandhi, and I found the whole experience both fascinating and humbling.

Street in Kyrenia

Kyrenia Harbour

Karaman Village

Women in Kereo Valley

Ty'r Eglwys

Building a dhow in Oman

Fishermen landing their catch, Oman

Dhows at Zanzibar

Cloisters, Cyprus

Luang Prabang Thailand

Enjoying village life in Cyprus

Pot making Burma

Street seller Vietnam

Minarets, Antalya Turkey

La Milcendiere

With the boys in France

My lovely daughter Sue

Family

Lovely Lamu

Our beach hut at Lamu

Market in Borneo

View from Shimla

Cooking for the thousands at Amritsar

The temple at Amritsar

The Laundry, Pembrokeshire

Mother Cheetah

Baby Cheetahs

Elephant crossing from Zimbabwe to Zambia

Indian character

Another Indian Character

Amber Fort

Tiger at Ranthambore

With Ben, Sam and Lauren in Cyprus

Final photo - 50th Wedding Anniversary

With my great granddaughter

CHAPTER 9

A new home in France

Back in the UK we decided to visit two dear friends of ours from our Cyprus life, Peter and Valerie Gough. The Goughs had also tired of the 'holiday/dinner parties' life of Cyprus and moved to France. Having always loved this country, we started thinking of buying over there and leaving the UK. So yet again we sold our house in the UK and started our search in France.

We stayed with the Goughs whilst we house-hunted and found the search long, arduous, and disappointing; we travelled all over Normandy and some of Brittany and were almost giving up when we were shown a property just outside the village of Le Teilleul, in Basse Normandie. It was sold as 'renovated' which was certainly not the case. Yes, the roof did not leak, the kitchen/bathroom was fine, but there was no central heating, an old cooker, paper thin carpet which had holes in it. However the location was superb! Set in three and a half acres, the views over the surrounding countryside and the village of Le Teilleul in the distance were breath-taking, and we fell in love with it.

Again, we continued our 'nomadic' life and moved over to France. We soon settled in, I brushed up on my French and we loved the French people, the life, and the country. Sue, who was fluent in French, was delighted that we had bought; she flew over from Thailand with the three boys and stayed for most of the summer holidays. We had a wonderful time, and the boys loved the huge expanse of garden. We visited Mont St. Michel, the medieval town of Domfront, the busy Wednesday market in St. Hilaire du Harcouet, the castle in Fougères. Sue helped translate to our neighbour, who was going to improve the outside patio area for us, and the Goughs, with their daughter Amanda and family, came for a barbecue.

All too soon it was time for Sue and the boys to leave and we drove to Paris to see them embark on their flight back to Bangkok. I can remember watching her leave with her three angels and there were tears on my cheeks. It was the first and last time she would visit us in France.

We started making our French house, which was already named 'La Milcendière de Bas', our home. We had already installed a lovely blue range cooker in the old fireplace alcove in the kitchen; the thin carpet in the lounge and kitchen was removed and John fitted wood flooring in the lounge. He was then tiling the kitchen floor. Already it was October, and I said that we really should register with the village doctor, so I made an appointment for the following day. Next morning Monsieur Madelin, our village plumber, arrived to start installing the central heating, and off we went to meet our new doctor.

Dr Seigneul was a charming man and very thorough. His surgery was in one of the village houses – no smart medical centre, but excellent service! We took our place in the small waiting room and when called, I went in first. There followed a thorough examination and I handed over all my medical notes. I then decided to go to the bank whilst John was being seen.

I will never forget his face when he met up with me. He looked shocked and just said, 'Like father, like son'. Immediately I knew what he was talking about. John's father had had an aortic aneurysm, though ironically, it never killed him – he died from a heart attack. I was shocked, obviously. We had to call back to the surgery and by this time, Dr Seigneul had spoken to the specialist in Avranches and we were to go there immediately. This we did, and after further tests, the specialist rang another surgeon in the large Rennes hospital. We were told to go there first thing the following morning and, in the meantime, John was to do nothing – not even drive the car. Needless to say, we had a sleepless night. I told both our children what was happening and said I would ring when I had news from Rennes.

After an early start the next morning I suddenly realised that John had been lifting boxes of floor tiles, and realised how lucky we were on two counts – firstly, the lifting could have made the aneurysm burst, and secondly our village doctor had detected the aneurysm in time. I drove the hour and a half to Rennes hospital just praying that nothing would happen en route. We found the hospital and met the wonderful surgeon, Monsieur Cardon. John was admitted and various scans and tests started. I, in the meantime, was alone in Rennes, knowing no one and not knowing where I would spend the night.

At the end of the afternoon, the lovely ward sister came to me and asked where I was staying that night. On finding out that I had nothing booked she told me to wait until she finished that evening and then I was to follow her in my car. This I did, and she took me into a sort of 'hostel' which was purely for the use of relatives of patients of the hospital, some of whom were long-term patients. I was introduced and shown my room – it was sparse but clean, and the bedding was there for me to make up my bed. This I did and went down for dinner, which again was very much 'all hands on deck'. The food was good, but I was the only foreigner there and therefore felt a little 'outside' and lonely. My French, though at that time not fluent, managed to get me by, but I was glad to phone the children and get some sleep. Sue and Nigel had discussed things and Nigel was coming over to be with me when John had the operation.

Luckily, the Metro had a station inside the hospital perimeters, so I was able to leave the car there, go into Rennes and find accommodation. There was an hotel right opposite the station, and I was fortunate to be able to book a room there and one for Nigel when he came. I shall always remember that first night in the hotel – there was no restaurant, but a few doors away I had spotted a Turkish restaurant. That first night, armed with a book for company, I went in and was immediately made to feel at home when I said 'iyi aksamlar' (good evening) and ordered my meal in Turkish.

Monsieur Cardon, at our initial consultation, had assured John that he would only have to have a small incision – I remember him saying, with his lovely French accent 'Ere in France, we do not do ze beeg cut, I will do a small cut'. But late that afternoon, following the scans etc, he returned and said, 'I am sorry, but I will 'ave to do ze beeg cut'. John had not one, but two aneurysms, a large one in the main aorta, which was at the point of leaking, and another, smaller one in the renal artery.

On the day of the operation Nigel arrived and was with me when we went to visit. I was prepared for the worst, but although in intensive care and with many tubes attached, John was awake and managed a smile – and I was SO relieved! A few days later Nigel left, while I remained in the hotel until it was time to take John home. It seemed to be providence firstly, in that we were living in France – in Britain you do not have a full examination when you sign with a doctor; secondly that Dr. Seigneul had found the aneurysm; thirdly, that we had such wonderful treatment.

During this time, I had been in contact with our lovely plumber, Monsieur Madelin, with whom I had left a door key. It was now November and John needed to go home to a warm house. Mr Madelin had finished the plumbing, cleaned up and left the heating on for us – I was so grateful and so happy to take John home.

We continued to make the house our home, and sadly, spent far too much money on it, sums that we would never recoup. New windows and some roof work, a beautiful conservatory etc etc, but then one has to remember that the alterations gave us pleasure, and we enjoyed living there.

That Christmas we had been due to fly to Bangkok, but obviously John could not now make the journey. We cancelled our flights and reserved some for the following March.

So in March 2006, having settled into our French life and begun to thoroughly enjoy Normandy, we went to Orly Airport and flew to Bangkok. On leaving arrivals we saw Sue waiting with her three gorgeous boys. They were SO excited; Oliver could not stop smiling and jumping up and down! It was so lovely to see them again. When we got to the house, however, I could immediately see that things were not right. Relationships were not good. There was obviously a problem, even though Sue tried to make excuses and cover up the truth. I wondered whether I should have said something. I am a firm believer in not interfering in marriage affairs, but now I do wish I had said something.

Sue put on a brave face, and sadly she was too proud to confide in me. I still remember the night the taxi was collecting us for our departure: Sue and Dan's close friend Andy was visiting from Malaysia, and he came outside with Sue to say goodbye. I shall never forget the way she clung to me that night – I cannot bear thinking about it, I still get very emotional.

On our return, we had the regular phone calls and chats about the boys. Then in April, just after her 41st birthday, Sue phoned. She was terribly upset, but tried to start a conversation before she started crying and said, 'Mum, it's back'. The cancer had returned, with a vengeance.

Our darkest days

The procedures started again – mastectomy etc. I begged, pleaded with her; John and I wanted to go over. I also asked her to come over with the boys, as cancer treatment in France was excellent. She was adamant and insisted that she was fine; friends were helping, and she kept emphasising that she did not want us to visit. She had also become epileptic and was on medication. I believe she signed herself out of hospital and insisted on going back to work, teaching at Shrewsbury. Then she had to go back into hospital, where they removed twenty-six lymph glands.

Again, back to work she went. I continued to beg her to let me go over, but she continued to stop me. Oh, how I wish I had just gone! I knew her friends were rallying around – Julie, Patricia... so many others. I believe the reason for her stopping me was that the marriage was breaking down and she did not want me to experience what must have been a difficult situation.

Late in September – I think it was the 28th, at about three o'clock in the morning – our phone rang. John answered. It was Julie, Sue's close friend, to tell us that our wonderful daughter had died. I cannot write much more about it as even now, almost fifteen years later, the pain is too great. She had died on the night of the 27th and had been at work that day. Too brave, too stubborn, too unselfish: these were the most horrible days of my life, and the loss and pain never goes. The only way I can describe how I felt is to say that it felt as if my inside had been torn out of me. I can remember when, after the funeral, Julie and I had to sort out her clothes, and, weeping, I said to Julie 'she should be doing this for me, not this way around'.

I will never forget the warmth and kindness we received from Sue's friends in Bangkok. Not only did poor Julie have the rotten job of telling us of Sue's passing, but she collected us from the airport. She and her husband Simon took us to where Sue was, so that I could love her and say my goodbyes: there were so many others, Trevor and Naree, Patricia and Mick, Jamie and Martin... so many. Two of these old friends, Andy and Laura, took the trouble to visit the boys every year in France, and later at our home in Wales. I apologise but I cannot name them all, it would take too long. Shrewsbury School was magnificent: they organised a memorial service for Sue and I am sure that there must have been several hundred people there, including a doctor who had treated the family. Afterwards the school had laid on a magnificent buffet in the grounds, but it was a very emotional day for us.

On a more positive note, Sue left us the greatest legacy that a child can leave her parents – our three wonderful grandsons. We have had them every summer for approximately eight weeks, and they lived with us in France for a term. I have done as much as I can for them and have tried to, in a pathetically tiny way, be a fraction of what their mother was/is to them. Oliver was eight and Ben was seven two days before Sue died, and we had celebrated Sam's fifth birthday the previous March when we had visited. I have a photo of Sam, riding on the elephant that Sue had arranged to come.

Life in France continued to be kind to us. John's health was fine, and he learnt a few words of French (enough for him to buy the morning baguettes). We had our dear friends Peter and Valerie (who had kindly taken our dog Anya when we went to Thailand), playing bridge with Roger and Tessa and good times with many other friends.

I am not sure of the exact time, whether it was at Christmas or Easter, when I felt so depressed that we took a holiday in Mauritius. It just did not work – the island was lovely, we had beautiful weather, but it was too soon after losing Sue. Yes, in a way, I enjoyed it, but there were times when I would suddenly burst into tears. I really cannot say much about that lovely island – I went there at the wrong time.

We had booked to go to Thailand in Christmas 2006, but were told not to come. I was desperate to see the boys, but I had to be content with regular phone calls and speaking to one of the maids to see how they were. I also spoke to Laura and Andy, who were visiting that Christmas, and to other friends who could assure me that our three grandsons were all right.

The following year Dan moved elsewhere in Thailand and the boys had to change schools. I managed to arrange for us to visit and take the boys on holiday. We were thrilled. The arrangement was that one of the maids would bring the boys to Bangkok airport, where we would collect them and then fly to Phuket. We had a wonderful holiday with them, and they enjoyed it so much! They needed some new sandals, new sun protection swimwear etc, so a shopping jaunt was the first thing we did. We also bought them snorkels, and this was the first time they had snorkelled – they loved it! We were staying in Julie and Simon's timeshare apartment at the Marriott Hotel and had a wonderful time there. It broke my heart when we had to leave them in the airport again, but at least we were able to love them and spoil them a little, if only for a short time.

After that they came over for the summer holidays. We would collect them and take them to Paris for their flights and for those eight or nine weeks we had wonderful times. We bought a children's quad bike – they loved that! There were trips to the Normandy landing beaches, the enchanted village at Juvigny, the Roman remains in Joublain, a zoo in nearby Brittany, and a trip to Futuroscope near Poitiers, as well as playing on the quad and building dens in the woods behind us. Some of these trips were taken when they lived with us, as Dan's brother, Tim, contacted us to say that Dan was moving to Dubai, where his brother was resident, and could we have the boys for a term? Naturally, we were delighted, but also concerned and worried. The boys would have to attend the village school – how would they cope? They spoke no French, which was going to be a huge challenge for them. However, there seemed to be no alternative, so once again, we were off to Paris to collect them.

After their arrival and the usual trip to the clothes shop they loved in Saint-Hilaire, it was time for them to start school. I knew they were nervous and apprehensive, indeed, who, in their position, would not be? I was equally nervous, if not more, but showed nothing of my feelings to them. I can remember explaining how, with the French education system, they would have two hours for lunch. I tried to break the day down into 'manageable' time slots, so that it did not seem so long for the boys to be away.

That first day, when I was waiting at 12 noon for them at the school gates, I was a complete bag of nerves and dreading what was to ensue. Amazingly, all three came out smiling, and I was SO relieved! The second day when I took them to school, they were happy and indeed, seemed to have made friends already – the truth is, I think, that our three were quite a novelty in the lovely village school of Le Teilleul.

So our lives settled into the school routine. They had just started their second week when I got a phone call from the headmistress asking me to come and fetch Ben, as he had fallen and hurt his arm. Over I rushed and took him immediately to see Dr. Seigneul (thankfully I had already registered the boys on the French medical system). On examination, Dr Seigneul said I would have to take Ben to the Saint-Hilaire hospital – he had broken his wrist and needed examination and probably a plaster cast. Off we went and yes, in his first week at school, Ben had his wrist and part of his arm in plaster!

A few days later the boys came home extremely excited. There was a 'cirque' (circus) in St. Hilaire, and people from it were coming to the school to teach them how to perform in a circus. Over the following days we were told that not only were they going to be taught, but they were going to perform in the circus tent!! Oliver was elated. He was learning, apart from other things, to ride a monocycle, and Sam was proudly learning to juggle. Ben, however, was not enthusiastic at all, as his arm forbade him from participating. He became very melancholy and sullen. When I tried to enthuse him and say that it would be fun to watch, he would pout and say, 'I am not going to the cirque'.

A few days later this pouting little boy came home from school with a beaming smile on his face and could not wait to tell me of the idea he had put to his teacher, and which his teacher had supported. Bless him, he had obviously thought a great deal about how he could participate and had come up with the idea of performing a mime wherein he was supposed to be the juggler, but his accident was making him constantly drop the ball.

The night of the cirque came and we, with many other vehicles, drove to the cirque. We took our seats inside the big tent whilst the boys, with all the other children, were taken to have their circus make-up put on. I must say, they did a magnificent job and the children loved it! Everything inside the tent went quiet, and we were told that the show was to begin. First on, to display his acting skills and introduce the acts, was Ben, miming to perfection the agonies felt by the juggler. He brought the house down – there was much laughter at this silly clown! The other boys in turn performed their acts, and I think it was midnight before we all got in the car to drive home – such a lovely experience for the children.

One of the highlights of living in Normandy is that there are so many medieval towns, and the one nearest us was Domfront. Each year they held a medieval festival, which was truly magnificent. People would dress in their medieval costumes, there would be jousting on horseback, jugglers and clowns, and exceptionally talented flag throwers. The first time they visited, the boys were fascinated, amazed and enchanted. This was the start of masks, imitation swords, shields, helmets and lots of duels between the brothers.

Of course, we also had visits from our other grandchildren. I remember one Easter when Lauren and William came on their own, and Nigel came, usually with one, two or three of his children; one year he came and brought over his new partner, Debi, for us to meet her and we had a pleasant holiday with them. Debi had brought her son, Ben, and we took the children riding at a stables near Mayenne. William played with our lovely Labrador, Ania, and like his cousin Oliver, he loved getting on John's sit-on mower and trying his hand at mowing the grass.

The following year I booked a large house with a pool further south in France and Nigel, Debi, Nick, Will and Lauren, together with Debi's son Ben, came over from the UK whilst John, the three boys and I drove south from Normandy. We had a super two weeks – good fun in glorious sunshine and good French food, plus barbecues and of course, wonderful wines and cheeses – a great family holiday.

The boys eventually left for Dubai, where their father and their aunt and uncle, Marion and Tim, resided. We missed them when they left, but they continued to visit every summer and when I think of living in France it is synonymous with having the three boys.

CHAPTER 10

Kenya, Malaysia, Sarawak and Borneo

The pull of Kenya

My thoughts turned once more to Kenya, for I longed to go back. Lauren was now about sixteen and living with Judith, her mother. I put my idea first to John, and with his approval, spoke to Judith to ask whether she thought Lauren would like to come to Kenya with us. Of course, Lauren was thrilled and excited about the trip. I spent quite some time in planning our itinerary and the time spent was worthwhile, as it was a fantastic holiday. It involved extra expense, as we had to fly to the UK to pick up and drop off our granddaughter. But after much thought, pricing, and deliberation I booked the holiday, and we flew business class with Virgin. I really wanted to show Lauren how wonderful Kenya was, and hopefully, to instil in her my love for that country, and moreover, my love of travel – in retrospect, I think I may have succeeded!

We landed in Nairobi and transferred immediately to Wilson Airport, where we were to embark on our one-hour flight to Siana airstrip (which was basically a clearing in the bush), but this was an easier and more comfortable way of reaching our destination and saved us three or four hours' travel. We had a while to wait for our plane, and I remember one of the Africans going to get us some sandwiches to eat whilst we waited.

On arrival there was no one waiting to greet us, so the pilot insisted waiting with us until we were collected. I urged him to go, but he insisted, saying that we would be easy prey for a passing lion! Then our hosts arrived in their four-wheel safari Jeep – two tall and handsome Masai, dressed in their brightly coloured cloths and adorned with beads and bracelets. We were to spend five nights at the Porini tented camp here. Lauren was both amazed and excited by the whole experience – I only wish I could afford to do the same, or similar trip, for all my grandchildren.

We were shown our tent. Lauren was sharing with us, and I think she was glad as she could hear elephants outside during the first night! We wanted to shower after our journey, and, as part of her African experience, it was good to introduce Lauren to the bucket or safari shower. In a corner of the tent was a small cubicle, and when we wanted to shower, we had to ask one of the Africans to bring down the buckets of warm water. In we would get, wash, and then order more buckets for the next person. Tented safaris, I believe, give you the most authentic African experience – you are more aware of the animals moving around you at night and realise you have to 'zip up' on leaving, otherwise the tent will be ransacked by cheeky monkeys. There is nothing like the feeling of drinking a warm coffee around a fire in the early morning before a safari; meeting and chatting with other camp residents whilst having your pre-prandial drinks around a roaring campfire – it's just wonderful, I almost feel as though I am there.

There followed five magical days. There were morning and late afternoon safaris and a walking safari where we were shown how to track and identify various animals and how to gauge how far away an animal or animals are. There was a trip to a nearby 'boma' (an enclosure used mainly for animals), and an evening drive with drinks served out in the bush, followed by a night safari. They were all wonderful experiences. Food was served in a large communal tent and was of an excellent standard.

From there we then flew to the lovely island of Lamu, off the Kenyan coast. Here I had rented a house for five days, and it turned out to be quite luxurious. After our return I learnt that the house was owned by one of the Monaco princesses! Lamu was, at that time, very unspoilt. However I describe it, however hard I try to capture the magic of that island, I cannot do it justice. You need to experience it: warm Indian Ocean waters; powder-like white sands; whitewashed houses covered in vibrant bougainvillea; the muezzin calling to prayer and the lovely donkeys that are the only mode of transport on the island. The lack of vehicles, together with the conservative, long-robed Muslim population, brings a sort of peace. It's an atmosphere that I have not experienced elsewhere, and I should love to return.

We stayed in the little fishing village of Shela. The house was perfect, its courtyard and rooms furnished with hand-carved Swahili furniture, its beds adorned with draped mosquito nets

– pure heaven! There were three lovely African staff to cook, clean and see to our needs. Benson, Douglas and Humphrey were charming and handsome. When walking around the village we came upon a silversmith, and Lauren watched as he carved her silver ring. Oh, how I wish to return to the beauty, peace and tranquillity of that magical island, where everything is done in a 'pole pole' manner – the Swahili term for 'slowly, slowly'.

The next, and final, stage of our holiday was to spend some days at a beach resort on the other side of Lamu island, an eco-friendly 'no shoes' haven situated on nine miles of white sand, its traditional thatched rooms with balconies situated near the water's edge. These 'bandas' each have their own bathroom and are furnished with a large four-poster bed. Leading off the bedroom is a covered veranda overlooking the sea. If Shela village was relaxing, this was the ultimate in peacefulness.

When we disembarked from the boat that had collected us from Shela, we went to meet our hosts, the owners of the resort. We were offered very welcome cold drinks in the thatched open bar/dining room by our host, Louis. He was soon joined by his lovely wife, Mary-Jo, and we chatted, saying that we had lived in Eldoret. Amazingly, they had both been brought up there, and although younger than John and me, they still knew many of the people we had known, and that night there was much discussion about people from Eldoret, where they were, what they had done, etc etc. The conversation was good, the company convivial, and the food excellent. Sadly however, I had by this time developed an allergy to large crustaceans, so I had to refuse the wonderful freshly caught lobsters that Lauren and John were devouring. We lazed, swam, watched all the crabs scurry on the white sand and waved to the Africans sailing by on their graceful dhows which carried goods into Lamu village. The highlight for John and Lauren was when Louis took them out on the boat and they swam with the almost tame dolphins, which let Louis give them a kiss.

On our return to Nairobi, I had reserved rooms in the Norfolk Hotel, long established and a regular meeting place for early Kenyan settlers. After dinner we all retired, as it had been a busy day. We were not flying until late the following day, and I wanted Lauren to experience 'Carnivores' restaurant in the city. We got there for a late lunch and really enjoyed the experience; we sampled as much or as little of the meats on offer as we wanted, and I seem to remember Lauren saying that the snake was delicious. I had declined!

All too soon it was time to return home, but it had been an amazing, wonderful, memorable holiday. The final luxury was when we were at Nairobi Airport awaiting our flight. One of the stewardesses came out and checked with me that we were three people travelling together and when I confirmed this, she told me that we were being upgraded to first class! It is the only time I have experienced travelling in such an elegant style, but we thoroughly enjoyed it, especially Lauren, who kept devouring scones and fresh cream in addition to the main meals!

Our usual French life continued. Often, we would go to the Wednesday market in St. Hilaire and have lunch amongst the 'local' workmen and others at an exceptionally good restaurant just outside the town. I still remember those wonderful, ridiculously cheap lunches, where you would have a choice of starters, choice of main course and choice of dessert, accompanied by a robust jug of wine for a total of approximately 10 euros! I am sure prices have soared since then, but the best part of the meal was when they cooked the locally produced steaks on the open fire – wonderful! Then there was the Le Teilleul market, and I remember one of the stalls was used by a local pig farmer who produced the best pork I have ever tasted. Furthermore, as the French never use the skin of the pig, he, on request, would bring it, beautifully scored, for me, so we had an abundance of pork crackling. We also loved the local baker, who not only produced delicious baguettes, but his patisserie was superb. How I wish I could have one of his mouthwatering 'tartes aux pommes' now!

Apart from the boys' annual visit, we saw the other grandchildren, as it was easy for them to fly over to Dinard Airport, where we would collect them. I can remember Lauren and William coming over at Easter one year: they were highly amused at the annual Le Teilleul pig race which took place in the centre of the village each Easter.

Malaysia, Sarawak and Borneo

The year was 2010 and Boxing Day that year was to be our 50th wedding anniversary. I had suggested that I rent a large country house somewhere, possibly in the sun, and the whole family (apart from the boys) could come with us. Debi was reluctant to leave her family, quite understandably, so that idea was quashed. I then discovered Pandaw cruises, small ships resembling paddle steamers but renovated to a high standard. On exploring destinations, I saw that they did a trip in Borneo, travelling up the longest river there, the Rajang, with lots of interesting stops en route, whilst allowing you to see parts of Borneo not easily accessible to tourists. I was immediately enthused and made enquiries. I eventually made a reservation, and we were looking forward to seeing new places and people, experiencing new cultures and ways of life.

We first had the long flight to Malaysia and then on to Langkawi, the largest of approximately a hundred islands in the Andaman sea. I had heard that Langkawi was beautiful, and it was, with pristine white sand and clear blue seas. We were there before the Christmas holiday and it was SO quiet – I think we saw only about eight other guests. It was an idyllic location and a good place to rest after the long journey. We lazed, swam and ate dinner by the pool with soft music in the background and the gentle sound of the sea – wonderful!

Rested and recovered from jet lag, we then flew to Kuching for a few days. Kuching is in the capital of the state of Sarawak, Malaysia. It is a fascinating city, small and uncommercialised, and it has a special atmosphere which enhances its extraordinary history. It was built up and ruled by the family of Sir James Brooke, the first of the 'white rajahs' who ruled Sarawak for over one hundred years. There are lovely, well-preserved old colonial buildings – John and I had our photograph taken at the entrance to the courts where Sir James married his wife, Margaret. The city has an historic waterfront, an impressive new Government building with its tall pyramid-shaped roof, a wonderful Chinatown and street stalls selling every spice you could think of. In India Street we passed a snake charmer, exhibiting his talent on the pavement and saw many locals busy shopping. Apart from spices, there were sacks and sacks of dried anchovies.

Whilst staying in this city we visited the nearby Semenggoh Orangutan centre, which was amazing. The orangutans are very much protected in the forest there, so they are living in their natural habitat and not restricted. Visiting is strictly controlled and is allowed only when the gamekeepers put food in a certain area for the animals to eat. I believe people are allowed in only once or twice a day and then just for a short period. They are amazing creatures, and it was a privilege to see them, though unfortunately, we had one camera and my battery failed! Perhaps that is a message that I need to return?

We then took a short flight to Sibu, in the central area of Sarawak. Here we were taken to our ship, aptly named the *Orient*, and met our fellow passengers over lunch. I cannot remember the exact number, but I think we were about 25-27 passengers. That afternoon we had a guided tour of Sibu, a very 'Chinese' city redolent of places like Penang, but without tourists. That evening we set sail for the Kanowit tributary, which leads up to the Rajang river. There was always something to see as we relaxed on the polished teak deck. We could watch people going about their traditional riverside life and saw the Iban tribe's longhouses – one, in particular, was of enormous length. These were all new sights, and extremely interesting.

The following day we arrived at Kapit, where we visited the museum and fort; the latter was built by Charles Brooke to stop the Iban from moving upstream and fighting with the opposing tribe, the Orang Ulu. On board ship we met some lovely fellow passengers. I am still in touch with one called Marilyn and her lovely daughter, Emma Louise, now a lovely young woman. The food was excellent and our cabins extremely comfortable – what more could one ask for?

We saw and did so much. We trekked through jungle identifying plants, getting on what was called 'the small Pandaw', a miniature of the main ship, to visit the famous Pelagus rapids. We visited a primary school and medical clinic in a small up-river community called Mujong. On our return, we pulled in at the side of the river and there awaiting us was the boat's chef and a few staff – they had prepared a wonderful barbecue. What a delightful way to spend Christmas Eve! One night some traditional Iban dancers came on board to entertain us, but for me, the highlight of the trip was when we were taken in a Combi van to visit some Iban people in their longhouse – it had 86 doors! We experienced the 'Miring' or offering ceremony and saw one of the elderly women weave a magnificent ceremonial blanket. We were also treated to a dance display and were able to see where they cooked their communal meals – all extremely basic, with earthenware pots over a fire. The women all seemed happy and contented and the children well looked after and cheerful. On the woven ceiling hung several scalps, a reminder that fifty years ago the Iban were head-hunters.

Christmas day came and apart from celebrations we experienced a mangrove cruise. The Christmas dinner served on deck was superb! Then it was Boxing Day, our 50th Anniversary. John had arranged for flowers to be brought on board, and we received a special breakfast and cards and congratulations from fellow passengers.

Our final stop that day was Sarikei, where we could wander around the old town square and the market and purchase any final souvenirs we wanted. Once back on board we were treated to a Chinese Lion dance performance on the quayside, performed by the students of the local secondary school. That evening there was a wonderful dinner and John and I were presented with a beautiful 50th anniversary cake. We were also given a special card featuring photos of us dancing on the previous night (we were not aware they were taking photos); all the staff and our fellow passengers had signed it, and we were also presented with champagne. It truly was a special anniversary.

The next day we sailed to Sibu and disembarked on the 28th December. We had had a wonderful holiday and a memorable anniversary. We flew back to the UK and then had a surprise celebration meeting with Nigel and family, which concluded an incredibly special time.

We returned to France in a snowstorm and were unable to drive our car up the slope toward La Milcendière. I was glad to be back in France, but John was, yet again, wanting to return to the UK. His health was slightly deteriorating and constant back pain meant that he could no longer play golf. He was not a French speaker and I think he was tiring of the maintenance of our grounds, even though we had help. The housing market in France was extremely slow, and we ended by selling our lovely home at a great financial loss.

CHAPTER 11

Welsh interlude

On first moving back to the UK we stupidly bought again in Rugby, thinking we would see more of the family, but that did not work out. Nigel had moved in with his partner and we hardly saw him. One highlight was that we had Nicholas living with us for a few months, which was great. I could not settle in England.

We then foolishly bought a static caravan in Ceredigion, Wales. I say foolishly, but we used it well – all our grandchildren loved visiting and we loved being back in Wales. The cost of keeping the caravan was not cheap, and we finally decided that we would sell it, and our Rugby house, and move back to rural West Wales.

The winter of 2012 entailed many visits to the area, despite bad weather! We travelled in torrential rain, fog, and snow, and eventually found, fell in love with, and bought an 18th century converted creamery/laundry which had been part of the Penty

Parc estate, just outside the small village of Clarbeston Road, in Pembrokeshire. With spacious rooms, magnificent Welsh slate floors, a walk-in inglenook and a farmhouse kitchen, this listed building captured our hearts.

So in February 2012 we moved into The Laundry, as it was named. As was our wont, we made improvements: they included a new shower, an en suite bathroom upstairs, plus an extra built-in wardrobe. wood flooring, and extra units and a range cooker in the kitchen. I loved the garden, especially the small 'secret' walled garden, and I loved living once more in the country. Whilst we lived in Rugby we had bought our lovely golden Labrador, Meg, and she loved Pembrokeshire, We had country walks and beach walks – it is such a beautiful, unspoilt area.

Nigel and family visited for John's 75th birthday at the end of May, and we were then looking forward to the boys' arrival in early July, but a few days before the boys were due John suffered a mild stroke – it happened early one morning when he went to the bathroom and suddenly his eyesight became different and strange. We both guessed it was a stroke and luckily the hospital was a short drive away in Haverfordwest.

I took him straight to A&E and it was later confirmed that he had indeed suffered a stroke. It had affected the right side of his brain and his peripheral vision was affected. This meant that he could no longer drive, and my husband was NOT a good passenger. He would persistently shout at me and tell me I was going to go into a fence, for instance, not willing to admit that his eyesight was distorting his vision. There were other changes. His memory deteriorated – I took over any 'business/banking' that had to be done – and he became irritable and short tempered, so it was, at times, difficult.

Despite all this, we still loved our house and being in Pembrokeshire. I had joined a book club in the village and we both joined the history society and made many nice friends. The boys arrived at Cardiff Airport, flying via Amsterdam, and were with us for nine wonderful weeks – their usual summer sojourn! They loved Wales and had a great time with beaches and barbecues, meeting relatives they had not seen, exploring the county and playing with Meg, who loved all the fuss!

Our property was one of several restored Penty Parc buildings, and sadly, one of them caused us great problems. The situation got worse and worse. They captured our dog and then rang the police to say she was attacking them, and they accused my husband of trying to kill one of them (this was when he was still driving). The police were constant visitors and it was making what should have been a perfect time extremely stressful. We considered selling our lovely home, but all that was delayed during the summer. The boys were again over for their summer break – Oliver had his GCE results whilst with us and was a great help to John, cutting the lawns etc. Apart from the neighbours, life was wonderful.

Then, one afternoon, we had yet another complaint which forced the police to visit (they were always sympathetic, and I think they were thoroughly fed up with all the fabricated stories). I asked the boys to give us privacy whilst we discussed matters. I said nothing, but suddenly I had pains across my chest: after the police left, I told John as the pains were continuing and getting worse. John insisted we went to the hospital and eyesight problem or not, he drove me there, after explaining to the boys and telling them to stay at home.

The outcome was that I had x-rays and was told I had to

stay in overnight. The following morning, I was visited by two doctors and was asked several questions – did I have a cough? Was I short of breath? I answered in the negative. I was then told that they thought I had some rare type of pneumonia. I was to go home, return in eight weeks for another chest x-ray, and if it was the same, then there would be further tests.

My fight with cancer

Of course, this was wrong. They should have done a scan that day, because as we all know, if it's cancer, delay gives it a chance to grow. The scan showed a tumour and after the usual scan/biopsy on the lung I was diagnosed with stage 4 lung cancer. I recently found the sheet I had signed giving permission for chemotherapy (I was given a 'cocktail' of pemetrexed and carboplatin). On the sheet is written 'palliative chemotherapy; benefits -symptom control; significant risks'. A handwritten addition to the printed risks was 'death'. When I asked what the usual life expectancy was, I was told 'about a year'. I signed the form the day after my birthday on 17th November, 2014. I started treatment the following day.

I could not believe that this horrible disease was striking my family yet again. My grandmother, my mother and my beloved daughter – it had taken them all, and I was determined to fight it for as long as I could.

The staff at Haverfordwest Hospital were wonderful, as was my oncologist from Singleton hospital. I had some ups and downs, mainly because of problems with my blood. I started on a trial, but sadly, when I had to have blood transfusions, they took me off it. I think I had three red cell infusions and then one white cell transfusion. The latter was rather amusing, as I had been in the cancer ward all day and it was about 4.30 pm when they took the tube carrying the infusion out of my arm. I thanked the nurse (some had already left for home) and started to walk out of the room. Suddenly I started to itch terribly and turned around to ask the nurse to look at my back. She looked and said 'Oh, my God, you have an allergic reaction!'. Oh, dear, I laugh now when thinking about it. Back in the chair I had to go, another cannula inserted, and another concoction to counter the allergic reaction! The poor nurse had to work overtime until the procedure was completed.

Generally, I coped well with the treatment, although the chemotherapy made me rather tired. Most days I still took Meg for a short walk, at least, as often as I could, and friends from the village, Geraint and Sheila, stepped in when I felt poorly. I was determined to live my life normally and to fight the disease. We had planned to go to Dubai at Christmas, as Ben was the only non 6th former taking part in the school play (ironically, he was, for the second time, playing the part of a jester or clown, Puck). Sadly, we could not go, but Oliver, who is so thoughtful, promised to send a recording of the performance, which he did.

I did not like the several biopsies I had, but I think the thought is worse than the event, as the staff make sure you are sedated enough to 'float' through the procedure. My oncologist was super, and so patient with me, as I was constantly researching online and asking endless questions. I continued life as normal and persevered with my walks. I remember people saying 'oh, but you don't look as though you have cancer' – I threatened to walk around with a big 'C' on my front!

I discussed radiotherapy with my consultant, and he organised for me to have radical radiotherapy – I think it was for a month – and it would be every weekday. As my husband could not drive (the treatment was in Swansea) I used the marvellous volunteer service. As the boys' visit coincided with the treatment, I asked if I could have morning appointments, so that I was at home to take them out in the afternoons. My consultant laughed, but he arranged that I only had morning sessions.

Actually, although sometimes quite a long journey, the volunteer taxi was quite fun as you would pick up and drop off other patients. I saw parts of Pembrokeshire I had never seen before and met a cross section of society. Some of the patients would be so funny, and others so miserable! While I was having this treatment, it was a huge help to have someone to walk Meg. I would leave at approximately 8 am and return between 2-2.30. Of course, this was six years ago – I don't think I would have the same energy today!

Since that time, you will not be surprised to hear, I have, yet again, moved to a new house, somewhere that is not so isolated and easier for family to get to – though I am still missing Wales and my house there. Just before I moved, at the end of July 2019, I had my regular scan in Haverfordwest. After registering with a doctor tere, I heard that Wales had messaged to say that my tumour had grown. It has always been difficult to see exactly what is going on inside my lung as the radical radiotherapy has basically made viewing difficult -apparently my lung looks like broken glass!

Again, I did some research and phoned the radiology department in Birmingham, where I knew they used the up-to-date cyber treatment. They said that if I was suitable they would certainly give me the treatment, and told me to speak to my oncologist and ask her to refer me to them. This I did, but my oncologist seemed reluctant to refer me to Birmingham, or to start the older, but basically similar treatment (called SABR) that they had at Coventry. I continued to have EBUS procedures (biopsy etc, CY and PET scans) and eventually she agreed that I should have this treatment – I am not sure what changed her mind. In November 2020 I finished the maximum number of sessions you can have, which is eight. For this I went to the excellent cancer centre in Coventry.

As for the results? We do not yet know. I have had a scan, but again, my poor lung is so used and abused that it makes it difficult for the radiographers to see what is going on, so as I write I am expecting to have another scan. I feel scanned out! Over the last few years, I have had so many: dye assisted scans, nuclear scans, biopsies etc. No wonder my poor body does not have the energy it used to have – but I AM ALIVE! I hope I shall live for several more years. This horrible disease has taken so many that I love, and I am not going to give in to it. Apart from that, I promised my daughter that I would look out for her boys, and I intend continuing to do so for a few years yet.! Also, the longer you can live, the more chance that they discover a new more effective treatment.

I would like to urge anyone who reads this who is diagnosed with cancer to fight, fight, fight! Please do not give up – there are new discoveries made all the time, so 'hang on in there' as the Americans say!

Enough of cancer (for the moment) – now to our next holiday.

CHAPTER 12

India: last holiday with John

After finishing my treatment and having the follow-up scan, I was anxious to enjoy every moment of life. Naturally, being an avid traveller, my thoughts turned to where we would like to go. One country we had not visited was India, so I suggested this to John. He was in agreement, and I started to plan the visit.

I had always wanted to visit Shimla, having read stories about the colonial era there: Rudyard Kipling's picture of Imperialist India; the talk of the theatre in the Mall; people walking and gossiping whilst strolling in this meeting place; the view of the Himalayas – all made it an interesting place to visit, and it had held a fascination for me for some years.

I was determined that this should be a fantastic holiday. Both John and I were aware that the future, and my longevity, was uncertain, so this was going to be a luxurious journey which we would enjoy and remember for the rest of our lives.

So, in September 2015, we flew from London to Delhi, where we were met by our driver and a guide. The first night we stayed at Claridges and we were treated like royalty! Flowers, a cake and champagne in our room – sheer luxury. We were given postcards already stamped for the UK should we want to send any home, and a mobile telephone with a number to ring should we need anything, medical or otherwise, whilst we were in India.

That afternoon we explored the Khan market, though the visit resulted in us making few purchases. The following day, after a good night's rest and a sumptuous breakfast, we left to fly to Amritsar.

Amritsar is famous for its magnificent golden temple, built in the sixteenth century. It is the holiest of Sikh sites and the city itself is named after the sacred tank which is inside the temple. We had been met at the airport by our driver and the extremely comfortable people carrier in which we were to travel; both would remain with us until we took our final train journey back to Delhi. Our driver was a delightful man – I am ashamed to say that I have forgotten his name. He was an excellent driver on hazardous roads, but as anyone who has visited India will know, there is no road etiquette, merely an excessive use of horns. He also gave us an insight into what it was like to be Indian in India. His wife and children were living upcountry, not far from Shimla, and he was determined that his children would receive a good education. We also had a guide, who would change several times.

That night we were offered a trip to the temple to witness the nightly Palki ceremony when the holy book is moved from its place inside the temple to its overnight room. I am afraid we declined – we were both very tired and just wanted dinner, some good wine and sleep.

The next morning, we left after breakfast, rested and refreshed and keen to see all that Amritsar had to show us, and we were not disappointed. I would recommend a visit to this city – it is fascinating. The temple is magnificent, built in white marble and copper gilt, its magnificent gold leaf dome glinting in the sun. We saw men bathing before they entered the temple; we solemnly bowed before the holy book of the Sikhs (the Guru Granth Sahib), and then we went into the huge community kitchen. I have never seen so many saucepans and dishes in my life, it was truly astonishing! We saw massive cooking pots filled with bubbling dal, and in another area there were women making hundreds of rotis (flatbread). Everything was spotlessly clean, and everyone looked so happy. Each day this kitchen feeds approximately 30 to 40 thousand people, and it is an amazing and a humbling experience.

Another humbling and moving visit was the next one we made, to the Jallianwala Bagh, which commemorates the hundreds of Indians killed or wounded by the dreadful massacre performed by the British. It really makes you ashamed of our dreadful colonial past.

This was, indeed, a full day, as we later went to the Wagah border, which is the border between Pakistan and India. The changing of the guard ceremony is performed with much pomp and pageantry, and even before the ceremony, we were treated to an impromptu display by Indian onlookers who decided to perform a dance to the music that was playing! We were surprised to see so many spectators on our (Indian) side of the border, but very few on the Pakistan side. I was later told that this was because in India viewing the spectacle is free, whilst on the Pakistan side they must pay to watch it.

The next morning, after breakfast, our driver was waiting to take us up country to our next stop, which was Pragpur. The drive was beautiful, with breathtaking countryside, plenty of holy cows having priority on the roads, families of monkeys sitting at the roadside and lorries blasting their noisy horns. We were on our way to Dharamshala, home of the Dalai Lama, but it was a long journey, and necessitated an overnight stop. After about five hours (we could take stops whenever we wanted), we arrived at our destination. A beautiful building, white walled and red roofed, stood in front of us and we were greeted by the owners of this delightful property. It was one of India's 'heritage' properties and the current owner was the son of the former judge who built and lived here. A charming couple, they asked whether we wanted tea or a cold drink, and then we were shown to our accommodation. Our room was in a separate building from the main house, and it was another residence, even though we were the only people there. The main hall was full of antique furniture, as was our bedroom.

We decided to walk through the lovely grounds and explore the nearby village, which again was charming. There were some old, dilapidated ruins, on which stood a 'holy' cow, looking at us as if we should ask permission to pass. We saw beautifully renovated buildings, shops selling spices and food, tailors busy on their sewing machines and cloths and saris on display. The children were coming home from school and all looked immaculate in their uniforms. Two students kindly allowed me to take their photograph – such pretty girls! We strolled back to the hotel/house and as we walked along the path in the grounds, we saw a group (I believe they are called 'colonies') of mongooses. On seeing us they scurried away, and I am afraid they ran so fast I was not able to take a photograph!

We had been told that there were to be drinks served on the front lawn that evening, and that a group of dancers was coming to entertain us. We duly attended for drinks and there were obviously other people staying at the residence as there were several tables, but where their rooms were, I do not know. We sat down and the barman brought our drinks, but the owner and his wife asked us to join them on their table. They were a delightful couple. He explained a little of his family history and how he had received a British education. The dancers arrived and performed, and we duly gave to the collection bag; the owner had explained that they were local dancers from the village we had visited, and he employed them to dance to supplement their incomes.

A delicious dinner followed, and we were then happy to retire for a good night's sleep as our driver was collecting us after breakfast the following morning.

The next morning, after our host had come to say goodbye and wish us a safe journey and a good holiday, we left for the approximately one-and-a-half-hour drive to Dharamsala, which is in the Dhauladhar mountains. It is now famous for being the home of the Dalai Lama, who moved there when invited by the then Prime Minister of India, Jawaharlal Nehru. He was offered a 'government in exile', and since then, several thousand Tibetan exiles have joined him. They mainly live in Upper Dharmsala, known as McLeod Ganj. It is also referred to as 'Little Lhasa' after the Tibetan capital city.

We were surprised that morning to see our driver had changed from his very smart white uniform and peaked hat into what looked more like a traditional outfit, made of heavy wool, and wore a warm winter hat. This was because, he explained, we were now approaching the highlands, and his previous summer uniform would not have been the correct attire for the colder climes.

The drive was extremely pleasant and the verdant countryside with many hills would not be the typical scenery many Europeans would think of as Indian. We passed rivers, small towns, steep inclines, lorries blasting their horns, monkeys galore and the ubiquitous holy cows strolling wherever they chose to go.

After this pleasant journey we arrived at our destination. We were to spend the night at Chonor House, a small hotel run by Tibetans. Although the room looked beautiful, I was somewhat surprised at the level of cleanliness – the room had obviously not had much of a clean before we arrived. The bedding was fine, so we ignored the rest!

Our driver then took us for a short drive to visit the 'British' Church of St. John in the Wilderness. Sadly, the Church was locked so we were unable to view the inside, which apparently had a magnificent stained-glass window and a tomb of one of the Viceroys of India. It was built in a neo-Gothic style and was very imposing, but it was in a wonderful, peaceful location surrounded by enormous pine trees. Our driver explained that there had been a huge army camp nearby and many of the British soldiers had succumbed to malaria in addition to normal army deaths. We wandered around the hundreds of gravestones and it was very poignant; I just wondered if any of the graves had been visited by relatives. It certainly wrapped you in a sense of peacefulness and was well worth the visit.

On our return to McLeod Ganj, John and I took a short walk along the main shopping strip and suddenly were engulfed by torrential rain. I can remember going into the shops and buying something – I think it was a traditional 'throw' or blanket. Sadly, I cannot remember what happened to it – perhaps I gave it away. It was obvious that the main inhabitants were Tibetan and the women, in their long, black sometimes embroidered traditional dress looked magnificent and impressed me with their gracefulness.

I am afraid that dinner in the hotel was not impressive. I cannot remember what we ate, but I have never, ever experienced such slow service. The following day I reported back to our guide, and I got the feeling that they had received complaints from others. Despite this, it is an experience I would not have missed, and they were such friendly people!

The next day was quite full. We visited the Dalai Llama's residence – unfortunately, he was not there. There are several floors to climb as it is high on a cliff overlooking the valley below. We also visited a beautiful temple, and the State Museum, where we watched artists painting – I remember buying one and giving it as a gift. There were also sculptors and pottery and an exhibition of anthropological items. Despite our disappointment in the hotel, we thoroughly enjoyed our stay there. Long before it became the residence of many Tibetans, it was the home of a huge British garrison which served the whole of the Kangra Valley – certainly a place not to be missed.

The next day we set off for Palampur. The scenery was magnificent, and we were climbing higher toward Shimla. The next night was to be spent at Taragarh Palace, a summer residence of the royal family of Kashmir. This forested estate was beautiful, surrounded by the tea plantations of the Kangra Valley, and is one of the most scenic and unexplored regions of Himachal

Pradesh. Located at a height of 1000 metres, the palace stands at the foot of the Dhauladar mountains, with views of the surrounding snow-capped peaks. We thoroughly enjoyed walking around the beautiful grounds here, but obviously the Palace was not now used regularly by the Royal Family, as many of the amenities needed maintenance or repair. The swimming pool looked tired, the tennis courts needed work on them, but the setting was magnificent. We enjoyed sitting on a balcony, with a cool drink in our hands and a good book to read. Outside our bedroom we could see the polo ponies – apparently the owner kept his finest specimens here when not being used. The staff were wonderful and the setting so peaceful. It was a memorable visit and so different from the normal busy impression one gets of India.

The final part of our journey to Shimla was to take approximately seven and a half hours, but we could, of course, make as many stops as we wished. I remember in one small town that we were passing through we stopped alongside a rural reproduction of the European 'take-away' and our driver bought us the most delicious samosas. We also stopped at a spotlessly clean roadside restaurant for lunch and were served bowls of very good dal and freshly baked pitta bread.

Shimla, formerly known as Simla, is the capital city of Himachal Pradesh, and at an altitude of 2,205 metres, it has views of the snow-capped peaks of the Himalayas. The air is fresh and clean, the houses/buildings arranged in tiers on the verdant hillside and the views over the valley framed by towering fir trees. My first glimpses confirmed why I wanted to visit this beautiful place, and I was so glad we had made this journey. The town is often referred to as 'the Queen of the hills' and rightly so, draped in the magnificent forests of pine, rhododendron and oak. The summers are pleasant, but the winters are cold and snowy. It was the summer residence of the British Raj in India and was a haven for the wives and children of British serving personnel who were in the hot and humid lowlands. The buildings here were fashioned in a Tudor and neo-gothic style, which again helped to make it unique.

When we walked down the famous Mall, it was easy to imagine the gossip that took place here (it was called 'scandal point'); it is reputed that there were many love affairs which took place with wives separated from their husbands. I had read of the Gaiety Theatre here, which was designed for the pleasure of the British residents – we were lucky, as it had only recently been re-opened after extensive renovation. We were allowed inside, but we were forbidden to take photographs. A magnificent, but small, theatre, its seating arrangements echoed the British class system, and I could just imagine the Viceroy and his wife sitting in their box, which naturally afforded the best view of the stage.

Our hotel here was the Oberoi, so again, a taste of luxury. We were looking forward to the second day here, when we were visiting the Viceregal Lodge. This was the place where the planning of the separation of Pakistan from India took place, with the boundaries decided on a world map. The building itself, and the grounds in which it is located, were magnificent, but the interior walls, decorated with magnificent wooden carving, were amazing! Everywhere we walked we got the impression of extreme opulence – it made me rather ashamed of how pretentious the upper echelons of British society were and how very different were the lives of rich and poor.

We had several days in Shimla. We visited temples, strolled along the Mall, saw a traditional wedding, and had the experience of travelling on the toy train from Shimla to Taradevi. This was another thing that I had wanted to do, but I am glad that our journey was relatively short, as the wooden seats on the toy train were not that comfortable.

All too soon we were coming to the end of our holiday and it was time to make the journey back to Delhi. As this necessitated an early start, the hotel kindly packed a very substantial breakfast for us before we left. We had been told that it would be better if we did not eat on the train! First, we had the four-and-a-half-hour scenic drive to Chandigarh, where we would board the express train to Delhi. Chandigarh is an extremely modern city and its excellent design is the work of that famous architect Le Corbusier. It is the capital of the northern states of Punjab and Haryana. Its impressive buildings and wide roads were in complete contrast to the architecture of Shimla.

We bade a fond farewell to our wonderful driver and boarded the Chandigarh Shatabadi for the four-hour journey to Delhi. The first-class trip was both comfortable and enjoyable, with much to see as we travelled. Staff came around with teas, hot soups etc. all included in the ticket price. It all looked good, but we did not partake after the warning we had been given – we had a long journey the following day!

Again, we were met at the thoroughly chaotic Delhi station, where your bags are speedily picked up by one of the many porters competing for work – you must endeavour to keep up with them! We were then driven to our final hotel, which was the conveniently situated Holiday Inn at Aerocity, Delhi. Another wonderful holiday had come to an end. It had satisfied a desire I had long held – to see Shimla.

It was also, sadly, and unbeknown to us, to be the last holiday

John and I would share. During the holiday I had noticed that John's pace of walking had slowed; he seemed to lag, and I would have to wait for him. Then there was one night when we were staying in Taragarh Palace and he missed dinner as he was not feeling well, but had no specific symptoms. We got home the first week in October, and for a while he seemed fine, although his appetite was diminishing and only certain foods appealed to him. His health steadily declined, and I got very concerned; I recognised symptoms I had seen with my mother. There were visits to the doctor, various tests etc, and in the December he was admitted to hospital. He had also lost weight, and always being quite slim, he could not afford to lose a lot. Despite all this he was happy and did not seem unduly worried, although I must admit, I was really concerned.

After various tests, the week before Christmas, his specialist came into the ward; I was sitting alongside John's bed. He asked us to go with him to a room at the end of the corridor. My stomach twisted – I knew there was bad news coming. We sat together and I held John's hand as we were told the worst. He had pancreatic cancer, which was inoperable. Of course, as I was a cancer patient in the same hospital, I knew all the cancer nurses. One of them came to discuss possible treatment, and we were to see the same cancer specialist who was treating me.

We spoke to the specialist the next day. Poor man, he looked as if he felt so awkward and sympathetic to have two of his cancer patients sitting in front of him who were husband and wife. John's case was discussed, and we talked of prognosis, and of the chance of any possible treatment. We were told that having chemotherapy might prolong his life, but there was nothing certain. As it was the only option we had, John decided to go for the chemotherapy, I think mainly because he had seen me receive the treatment and benefit from it. I took him to the hospital for two sessions of treatment, but, after realising that it was not working, we discussed matters and John decided to stop the treatment.

I hate to recall how quickly, and to what extent, he deteriorated. He lost so much weight. Trying to get some nourishment into him was hard. He was bedridden, and oh, dear, I have to smile when I think of how I used to get him on to the commode or change him. I am not a large person, but he would have his arms around my neck and cling on – we would do it in stages, with me saying 'one, two ,three' and then by him trying to move with me, I managed to get him from one position to another.

For the last few months, we moved from our upstairs bedroom to the downstairs one. I often think how lucky we were to be living in the laundry, where we had this facility. I cared for him to the best of my ability and during those last few months we constantly spoke of love – I am so glad that we did. Lying in his bed (he hated the fact that he did not have the strength to stand and see to himself) he would look at me and say, 'you are doing everything for me, aren't you, love?' To which I would reply, 'that is what a wife is for, and I want to do it'.

The suffering grew worse, and he was desperate to die. He was constantly telling me of his wish, and he repeated this to the nurse who called. His dose of morphine was increasing to ease the pain and he would get so restless and almost aggressive during the night. I would be in and out of bed, administering the drug, and making a note of when and how much he had.

As time went on, a local cancer charity called Paul Sartori became involved, and they were fantastic. They insisted that I should have an afternoon off once a week, which I did, and they would attend to John. The trouble was, although I took the opportunity to go out, I could not relax, and would always be home before the due time.

He was approaching his 78th birthday, which was at the end of May, and when the nurse called one day, he pleaded again, 'I want to die'. He also said that he would never reach his 78th, to which I laughed and said that of course he would.

I remember that we had some hot weather and while he was sleeping in the afternoon, I would sit in the study, which was near the bedroom, and leave both doors open, while I collated photographs to make an album of his life and our life together – I could think of nothing else to give him as a gift. The day came and he looked at the album and said, 'where did you get all these photos? This is wonderful'.

He looked at the album twice; after that he was too weak. He died, at home, with me lying beside him, holding his hand, at 1 am on 13th June 2016. He was at peace after months of torment. Sometimes death is a blessing.

One thing I remember was what our lovely doctor said to me the first time he saw me after John's death. He said that the nurses had commented on how much love was in the house. That meant, and still means, a lot to me.

Following the funeral, and after all the family had left, it was difficult to adjusting to being alone; I still find it very difficult. One has to adjust and keep busy. I also had friends I could call on, which helped enormously. The three boys, Oliver, Ben and Sam, came for the summer holidays and, as always, they filled my days. The weather was good, we explored more of Pembrokeshire, visiting bays they had not previously seen, a trip to Cardigan and viewing the castle, the Neolithic burial chamber of

Pentre Ifan, Carew Castle etc. Pembrokeshire is such a wonderful county, and providing you have nice weather it equals anywhere in the world!

CHAPTER 13

Cyprus, alone

The following year I wanted to take a summer holiday and thought it would be nice to visit my old home in Northern Cyprus. I asked some of the grandchildren, namely Sue's three boys (who always spent the summer holidays with us) and Lauren if they would like to come. They all jumped at the prospect and I booked two rooms in a central Kyrenia hotel.

We had a wonderful time. It was many years since the children had been there and a lot of the memories had faded for them. It was such a pleasure for me to re-awaken those memories and see the happiness in my grandchildren's faces! I reintroduced them to lamacun, the Turkish-type pizza; bulghur kofte was a favourite lunchtime snack. There was a trip to Bellapais and also Kyrenia Castle, and we swam in the pool and took a trip in a gulet (a classic Turkish sailing boat) along the coast – the boys loved diving off the boat into the clear, warm Mediterranean Sea. We were able to meet up with the boys' aunt and uncle, Tim and

Marion, and their lovely daughter Jess. Tim and Marion (Dan's brother and wife) lived in southern Cyprus and came over for an afternoon and evening. It was lovely to catch up with them and we had a delightful meal together in Kyrenia Harbour. All too soon it was time to return home, but I thoroughly enjoyed the holiday and the company of my wonderful grandchildren. I am sure they enjoyed the whole experience.

Indeed I decided, yet again, to take them back the following year. They were all delighted to come, apart from Oliver, who was now in a relationship with Olivia. generally called Liv. I also think he thought himself too adult to be holidaying with his gran! That year I reserved rooms in a new, very smart hotel which had a private beach and several pools. We had a wonderful time! I can still remember Sam's face when we drove into the hotel. It was at night and when he saw the lights adorning the trees outside and the huge marble foyers when we entered, his delight was obvious. The food at this venue was excellent and much to Sam and Ben's liking, there was always a gentleman making fresh sushi – with no limit on the number of helpings!

All the food was of a very high standard and we enjoyed everything: revisiting the harbour, meeting up with Marion and Tim, swimming in one of the three pools or at the private beach. We also did a trip to the Karpaz, but although still lovely, the trip was disappointing for me. We stopped at a small cove, not the magnificent nine-mile beach; the route up was on the new road, not the old way I had been used to; the donkeys were there, and the lovely monastery, but I could see it was all changing and I wondered if they have started building big hotels. If so, it will not have the same sense of seclusion, the feeling of being 'away from it all' that we were fortunate enough to have all those years ago.

Tim kindly drove me to Karaman, to see Sue's old house and the new one we had built. Sue's house still looked beautiful, and I would have loved to see inside – the position was still spectacular and the village unchanged. Sadly, when we drove down to see our old house, 'Cloisters', all was different. When we built, we had been the only house down there. Later, we had a few neighbours, two of whom (Don and Daphne) I am still in touch with. Now, however, there were houses as far as the eye could see, possibly as far as Zeytinlick. The entrance to our house had changed and it all looked different, and I was disappointed. Girne (Kyrenia) had also changed. It had a new road system which made areas unrecognisable to me and they had started to erect high-rise buildings – always a sign of change. In some people's eyes it's a sign of 'progress', but to me, it's a sign of anonymity – it destroys the character of a place. It always reminds me of the satirical John Betjeman poem entitled 'Inexpensive Progress'.

Nevertheless, we had a good holiday, and I remembered enough Turkish to be able to haggle a lower price for the gulet trip, which highly amused the grandchildren. That was to be the last holiday with them, although the boys still spend a lot of time with me (apart from the last year with Covid and isolation). They were all now adults and too old to spend holidays with an ancient like me, and that is how it should be. It was now time for me to enjoy Wales, my lovely house and garden and my friends in Pembrokeshire.

My son continued to urge me to move closer to him in Warwickshire, but I resisted. I continued to have my regular check-ups, scans etc. The staff in Haverfordwest were always super – I now knew most of the nurses on the cancer ward. I especially remember Kirsten, who was the senior nurse in that area – I knew her so well, she would often give me a hug before I left. I was reluctant to leave my lovely home and the lovely friends I had made: Sheila and Geraint, who had adopted Meg and loved her as much as I did – they still brought her to visit me; Cliff, my neighbour who lived at the bottom of the hill, who would come for a glass of wine or invite me to his home for the same and we would have long discussions and set the world to rights; my lovely friends in the book club – we met in the village pub and talked about everything apart from the book we were reading; and the members of the village historical society – such interesting talks and wonderful archaeological visits. I was loath to leave this small friendly community, but instead I decided to focus on my home.

Despite all the alterations and updating John and I had done, I still wanted to do more. Our wonderful carpenter put high skirting board where it was missing; he constructed and fitted tall shelving in the inglenook to hold all the logs; I had the lounge decorated and finally the expensive replacement of four sash windows. They were made in wood, double-glazed and painted the same dark red as the rest of the house. The local craftsman who made them did a superb job, and I loved them. I intended staying in Wales.

Again my thoughts turned to Africa and I nervously made a reservation with a well-known holiday firm who focused on older clients; I was going on a 'singles' holiday to a part of Africa not yet visited – Zimbabwe. I was leaving in November and although apprehensive about travelling alone I was SO excited at the prospect of seeing both the famous Victoria Falls and the game and scenery that country promised. We flew Ethiopian Airlines, which was excellent, except for the change in Addis Ababa

– I have never experienced such a chaotic airport! It seemed that the whole of Africa had accumulated there. I spoke to people going to Kenya, others going to Botswana, some to Namibia – it was obviously, the changing point for most of Africa! Chaotic, but atmospheric, and I spoke to some charming Africans who, with their lovely smiles and friendly chat, made the whole experience pleasurable.

We were a small group of travellers, which made the holiday so much nicer. When we landed at Victoria Falls airport – it was only opened in 2016 – we were greeted by our guide, Mike. We could not have asked for a better guide – he was superb! I was rather surprised that we had been able to fly directly into Victoria Falls – it made our journey so much shorter, and it was very convenient.

Escorted by Mike and an African driver, who again, was friendly and turned out to be both an expert driver and an even better game spotter, we were taken to our first stop at Batoka Gorge. The gorge was 22 kms from the falls and the lodge we were to stay in for a few nights was beautiful. We were welcomed by the hospitable husband-and-wife owners, and after a welcome drink and introduction, we were shown to our rooms. I say rooms, but they were individual lodges with excellent facilities. It was positioned 200 metres above the Zambezi river, and the views over the gorge were beautiful. Our rooms were furnished in the lovely African style – big double beds adorned with mosquito nets, which to me not only epitomise Africa but provide a good, protected night's sleep. Off the large bedroom with its waxed wooden floor was the bathroom, but outside was another shower-room and toilet. The lovely outside veranda housed a small outdoor 'plunge pool and the views from there were beautiful!

That night we were treated to a virtual banquet and the owner then gave us an interesting talk on the rare Verreaux eagle. The next day we were fortunate enough to see this magnificent creature – one obligingly flew past, exposing its magnificent 7-8 feet wingspan. We saw a pair of these wonderful birds as they swept down to the gorge below to feed on the hyrax which lived on the rocks there.

That day we were taken to Victoria Falls, place I have always wanted to visit. We were there at the wrong time of the year to see the Falls at their fullest, which is between February and May, but even in November they were magnificent. We walked along the edge and could look over to the Zambia side and the area where people swim, apparently safely, but it is not an experience I would test! Even at that time of the year the spray was strong. Some showed on my camera screen, and I wondered how people manage to take photographs in the high season!

The falls were discovered on the date of my birth, in November 1855, by the famous Dr Livingstone, whose statue is placed nearby. I must say, looking at his statue, I would estimate that he was not a man not to be argued with! The falls itself -called, by the locals 'Mosi oa Tunya' is an extremely eloquent description which means 'the smoke that thunders'. Twice as wide and deep as Niagara Falls, apparently 440,000 litres of water pass through every second. I am so glad I visited – I would gladly go again to see the falls in their full splendour.

After this we went to look at one of the oldest trees in Zimbabwe, one which Livingstone had visited. Then we were able to do some shopping and saw the railway that links Zimbabwe to Zambia. It's the only bridge in the world that can be used by trains, cars and pedestrians. That afternoon was concluded with a lovely afternoon tea at the famous old colonial Victoria Falls hotel.

That night we were treated to a marvellous barbecue at the lodge, and we retired after another splendid day, knowing that the following morning we had an early start to reach our next destination – Hwange National Park.

After an early breakfast, we left for our road journey to Hwange. The drive was pleasant and interesting, and we eventually arrived at a small railway station – I say small, it certainly was, and there was no one in sight. Then a single open carriage truck arrived. I think it accommodated twelve passengers and on its rear was proudly printed 'The Elephant Express'. On we climbed and Mike, our guide, together with our driver, started handing out sandwiches and cold drinks, whilst we enjoyed looking at the surrounding game park and keeping a watchful eye for game. On the way in, we saw some graceful giraffe, impala and some cheeky warthogs.

Finally, we arrived at our home for the next week – or was it ten days? Whatever the length of our stay, I would have liked longer! It was called Bomani lodge and there was a warm welcome awaiting us. The safari drives here were magical, and we did day, early morning, evening, and night drives. We would emerge from our rooms in the morning and go toward the central communal thatched room/hall. Just outside was a roaring fire and around it were set our chairs. There was delicious porridge being made on the fire, and the kettle was boiling for tea or coffee. Alongside was a table laden with fruit, yoghurts, cereals etc and as much breakfast as one wanted. Early mornings are cold in Africa, so the warmth of the fire was a welcome feature.

Hwange is the largest game park in Zimbabwe and is known

for its huge elephant population -more than 44,000. However, the rangers have an enormous task protecting them, as there is easy access over the border from Zambia, and even the elephants stray across via the mighty Zambezi river. It was horrible to see how many snares had been found – a cruel, heartless way to capture and kill these lovely creatures for human greed. It is time the world took notice of the decline in numbers of these and other animals – we are depriving the planet and future generations if we do nothing – or even not enough!

We took an evening safari on one occasion and drove to a large waterhole. Our driver parked away from the water, in such a position as to prevent the herds knowing we were there. It was wonderful to see so many coming, males, females and young, all enjoying the water. On another occasion we watched hippos snorting in the water, opening wide those enormous mouths and surrounded by their young. We saw so many animals: cape buffalo, saddle-billed storks, warthogs, giraffe, cape buffalo, baboons, monkeys and the horned gnus, etc. There were also lions, and on one night safari we saw a pride on the hunt.

However, for me, the highlight was the day our driver stopped near the railway track. We could not believe our eyes when out of the bushes strode a beautiful, lean cheetah, accompanied by her four darling cubs. This magical creature got to the railway crossing, rested her front paws on the rail and surveyed the land on the other side. Her young kept close to her, and she then sat between the rails and continued to survey the land. The four cubs jumped up and nestled between the sides of the railway; their mother must have signalled to them to stay, as she then jumped off and went in search of food (we thought she had spotted some impala) while the four cubs cuddled in together between the tracks. We were spellbound, sitting in our vehicle just mesmerised by the sight and antics of these four siblings. After about fifteen minutes they must have started to be afraid – one of them sat up and made a strange call and the mother, in the distance, responded. All four immediately jumped up and went to join her. What a wonderful, rare experience – we were so lucky! I had seen cheetahs many times before, but never so near.

All too soon it was time to leave Hwange and move to our final destination, Gwembe Lodge at Zambezi National Park. This was another magnificent lodge with luxurious accommodation and a superb location overlooking the Zambezi river. Again, more safaris, more excellent food – and when walking to the central dining room, I had to pass by several tame young buck!

I remember one day there was a power cut, and the owner was desperately trying to get the electricity working. He explained to us how difficult things were in Zimbabwe now. We were aware of the current situation, because we had seen people queuing for miles and miles to get petrol for their vehicles, though often by the time they got there it had all gone. Prices, even for basic necessities like bread, had gone through the roof. This was after Mugabe's time, so goodness knows what it had been like before! The Europeans who had stayed there under Mugabe obviously really loved Zimbabwe and Africa to live with such hardships and so, so many frustrations.

Again we had game drives and here we were able to take a boat trip on the Zambezi. Such a wide, magnificent river – not only did we see many hippos on its edge, but a troupe of elephants crossing from Zimbabwe to Zambia – they did not need passports! Due to the proximity of Zambia at this point, the massacring of elephants was particularly bad.

We were also given the opportunity to canoe down the river – I declined, as I did not think I could cope with any fast-flowing rapids! I was more than happy, however, to partake in the lovely boat trip on the river and be served evening drinks whilst we watched the magnificent sunset. On one occasion I and several other ladies decided it would be nice to dip our feet into the Zambezi: we found a shallow rock pool on the edge, sat down and enjoyed the cool water on our feet. One of the group, Jenny, took a photograph of us, and it was only when we looked at that did we realise that not far from us, obviously awaiting the right moment, was a crocodile!

Towards the end of our stay here I was awoken one morning at about 6.30 by Mike, our guide, knocking at my room door. He had been told that there were lions feeding on their kill not far from the lodge and he was asking if anyone wanted to drive to view. I quickly got dressed and there was one other from the group who joined, so off we drove with Mike and our lovely African driver. We found the location, but unfortunately the lions had left, although we managed to see them as they almost crossed our path – there were two of them, a male and female. By the time we reached the kill all we saw were many vultures -some greedily eating the remains that were left, whilst others hovered in the tree above, waiting to swoop and devour the remaining morsels of what had been a zebra, its rib cage sadly protruding.

Like most people, I dislike vultures, but they are a necessary part of nature and come in a variety of species. Unlike hyenas, they do not generally kill, but feed on what remains after other predators have finished. They have almost bare heads, which apparently is nature's way of ensuring that they have no feathers to get entangled with remains when they reach inside carcasses.

Nature always amazes me – we have so much to learn!

That was my last morning in Zimbabwe, as after breakfast were taken to the airport for our departing flight. I love Africa, and Kenya especially, but I also loved Zimbabwe and would like to return.

CHAPTER 14

Settling in the Cotswolds

We arrived home just in time for Christmas 2018; I cannot remember where I spent it – probably with Nigel. In 2019 I eventually gave in to family persuasion and put my lovely home up for sale. Despite being a lovely home in a peaceful location, it took a while to sell. Many people when they move to Pembrokeshire want to be near the sea. I had several viewers who loved the house but wanted a coastal location. I did, however, after much stress, eventually sell and moved to the Cotswolds on 29th July, 2019.

Although Nigel wanted me to move to Warwick or Leamington, I chose Shipston-on-Stour in the North Cotswolds, a smaller, quieter town, which had all the facilities I needed, plus, the information said, a vibrant U3A group. I had been a member of U3A in Wales and after John died, I found that being able to join groups, eg for bridge, was a life saver. But I found the move traumatic. I had done everything alone, and as anyone who has moved to a new house knows, it is a nerve-racking experience, and worse when you are alone. I really think I came to the point where I was on the verge of a nervous breakdown, but I survived, and if you can fight cancer you can cope with anything.

I settled in to a new house with no work needed, but also none of the character I love. I still have to keep telling myself I have done the right thing and I know I have, but oh, I miss living in Wales and being able to walk on the beach, and I miss the quiet of the countryside! Nevertheless, I joined the bridge club here and volunteered myself to run a French conversation group. I have met some lovely people and made some good friends – life without friends would be no life!

I then decided that I would like to be away for Christmas – despite nice friends I was alone and felt I would prefer to be in the company of other single people. I was attracted by another, different 'singles' holiday firm and decided upon a trip to another part of India which I had not visited.

I decided to take the trip to India's 'Golden Triangle' (Delhi, Agra and Jaipur) and looked forward to it immensely. At the airport I met my fellow travellers, who were all extremely nice. There were five men and, if my memory serves me correctly, nine women, including myself. Sadly, the holiday was very badly organised: where we should have had internal flights, we were either transported by bus or train. The travel arrangements were abysmal. Each day, except for one, we were up at about 3.30 am. I think on one 'lazy' day we got up at 7 am. Breakfast was usually uneatable – a pack of dried-up sandwiches and a piece of unwashed fruit. Being India, one is careful with food and consequently most 'breakfasts' ended in the rubbish bin!

Prior to the holiday, I had read that Delhi had been suffering from excessive smog, so I rang the holiday firm and explained that I was concerned because of my lung cancer. I was told that the smog had cleared and there was no problem. We arrived in India to a Delhi smothered in smog, and road barriers everywhere due to political unrest!

Despite all the bad things about the holiday, we saw a great deal, we were a jolly crowd who made the best of a bad situation. A friend messaged me whilst I was there and said, 'how much are they paying you to go on this holiday?' That sums it up – but there was nothing we could do to make the situation better. The sights we saw were amazing, but it was spoilt by the organisation and the abysmal weather. Not only was there smog, but it was SO cold!

One of the nicest, warmest days we had was when we visited Madhya Pradesh and saw the Kama Sutra temples. The grounds of the temples were well manicured and verdant and the temples beautifully and intricately carved; most were adorned with highly erotic scenes and figures. It was extremely interesting, and we enjoyed the warmth, but the return journey was long and tiring, as we left our hotel early in the morning and returned very late at night.

We saw some wonderful sights, including Amber Fort, with its magnificent sandstone walls, perched high on the hill overlooking Maota Lake below. Built on four levels, each level having a central square, it is certainly a beautiful building, with perfectly planned gardens and an area built for the females, who could look out through the small gaps in the structure, but not be seen from outside. We stopped at Jaipur's palace of the winds, another beautiful building constructed of red and yellow sandstone.

There was a visit to the Taj Mahal – the most famous building in the world, known to have been constructed out of love. It was truly magnificent, but, as you would expect, very crowded. It is, of course, a mausoleum, built for the emperor's favourite wife when she died. Built of ivory, it is uniquely beautiful.

The highlight of the holiday for me was our visit to Ranthanbore National Park, where we were taken on several safari drives. There were deer galore and many species of wading birds, some with magnificently coloured plumes, and we even saw a crocodile. We were, of course, in search of the elusive Bengal tiger. The weather was atrocious – so cold, and we were all wrapped up with woolly caps to keep our ears warm. Then, on Christmas day, we did see a tiger! He was magnificent and we were extremely fortunate to see him, and at close quarters.

Another memorable evening was when back in Delhi, before our return, we went to the Ganges to witness the nightly Hindu Arti ceremony, performed by waving lighted lamps whilst singing and chanting prayers. By the time we got there it was dark (and very cold), but after watching the ceremony we went a short distance away, sailing on the Ganges in a small boat. There, on the banks, were families lighting fires around the bound bodies of their dead relatives. Like many other societies, death is far more accepted in India than in many Western societies.

My final, endearing memory of that night is when we started to make our way back from the river to board a tuk-tuk to take us back to the hotel. The alleys leading up were extremely dark and very uneven – it was easy to trip and fall. A young man came to me and offered his arm – he was deaf and dumb. Gently he made sure that I missed all the potholes and was aware of the steps as he held my arm and guided me. When we got to the road, I gave him some money and thanked him; rather than leave, however, he insisted on seeing me back to the tuk-tuk, on our way showing me where he and a few other dumb people lived. He managed to convey that there were four of them, and that he was now married. His gentleness and kindness made me feel so humble; he looked so poor, yet he was so kind. When we got to our destination, I offered him more money, but he refused. People like him make one look inwardly, give thanks and try to be a better person.

I can hardly believe that I took that holiday at Christmas 2019 – how little did we imagine what would come in 2020. The pandemic has affected us all, some more tragically than others. So many have died, and so many are still dying. In other countries, especially India and Brazil, there were soon thousands dying every day. Some countries, in the southern hemisphere have hardly been touched – they have been able to live 'normal' lives, whilst the rest of the world lives an alien life, masked, segregated. Isolated and afraid – afraid to shop, afraid to touch, afraid to hold. On a personal level I have never felt so alone, and so lonely. Thankfully I have good friends, with some of whom I play on-line bridge; one couple, Ron and Bobbie, who were in my French group, have been such true friends. They have been in my 'bubble' and with them, and through their kindness, I have somehow just kept my sanity.

I hear the news and it is all so depressing; society seems to have gone mad. There are protest marches about so many subjects – race, policing, sexual abuse – and then there were the terrible riots in Northern Ireland. Was this happening because there was a need to protest, or were these protests linked to the pandemic? The majority of protesters seemed to be young, and I think that the loneliness felt by many young people, the change in the world around them, the inability to socialise in clubs, pubs etc made a huge impact and was, to some extent, to blame. Let us hope and pray that in Britain, in 2021, we are beginning to get our lives back to some sort of pre-pandemic normality.

As for the rest of the world? We cannot guess, but we can only hope that vaccination will reach all populations, that by 2022 this pandemic will be controlled, and the world will be more prepared for such future catastrophes. As for holidays, I wonder if, and when, I shall be able to travel again.

This year I shall reach the age of eighty. I have had a good life - not without sadness, but also with joy. I suppose one has to have one in order to appreciate and enjoy the other. Life alone, despite having good friends, can never replace having a partner: someone close to discuss things with, to agree/disagree, to love and to comfort, to share with and travel with. I, and I am sure many others, miss this.

I am, however, extremely lucky: lucky to be surviving cancer (at least at present); lucky to be able to look after myself – many at my age are unable to do so; lucky that I can afford to go on holiday.

I only hope that my grandchildren will find happiness in their lives. I hope they will enrich them with travel; I hope they will realise that money and possessions do not give happiness and that the most important thing in life is love – love and care for others.

Finally, I sincerely hope that the recent treatment I received will give me another six years – as long as they are good years, years in which I can travel and see places I have yet to visit – New Zealand, Cuba, Bali, and, of course, Africa, the land where I left my heart so many years ago.

Printed in Great Britain
by Amazon

63848680R00132